CRAIGDARROCH

The Story of Dunsmuir Castle

Terry Reksten

ORCA BOOK PUBLISHERS, VICTORIA, B.C.

Fifth printing, 2000

Canadian Cataloguing in Publication Data

Reksten, Terry, 1942-
  Craigdarroch

    Bibliography: p.
    Includes index.
    ISBN 0-920501-07-9
    1. Craigdarroch Castle (Victoria, B.C.) —
History. 2. Victoria (B.C.) — Buildings,
structures, etc. — History. I. Title.
FC3846.8.C7R44 1987   971.1'34   C87-091204-6
F1089.5.V6R44 1987

Financially assisted by the Government of British Columbia through the British Columbia Heritage Trust.

Orca Book Publishers
P.O. Box 5262, Stn. B.
Victoria, B.C., V8R 6S4

Typeset by AMS Graphics, University of Victoria.
Printed in Canada by Hignell Printing Ltd., Winnipeg, Manitoba.

To James Knight Nesbitt and all the members of the Castle Society who continue his work.

Archivists and librarians have been as helpful as ever. I would particularly like to thank Kathy Bridge at the Provincial Archives of British Columbia and Ian Baird of the McPherson Library.

Thanks are also due to Bruce Davies, curator at Craigdarroch, who allowed me free access to his own research and to the castle archives; to Rita Hammett who opened the archives of the 'College Room' to me; to Geoff D'Arcy who shared his reminiscences of Victoria College; to Phil Simpson who allowed me to use his own castle research; to Peter Scott who shared his information about the Dunsmuir family and who was ready to spend hours discussing theories; to Candy Wyatt and Carolyn Smyly for proofreading and copyediting; to Don Reksten for copying many of the photographs; to Stuart Stark for designing the cover; and last, but not least, to Bob Tyrrell who came up with the idea for this book and who endured missed deadlines with uncharacteristic patience.

CONTENTS

Introduction

Even today, more than one hundred years since its construction began, Craigdarroch Castle continues to dominate Victoria's sky line. A dream-castle, a fantasy of soaring chimneys, towers and turrets, steeply-pitched red-tiled roofs and exquisitely crafted stained glass windows, Craigdarroch remains unchallenged as the single most expensive residence built in Western Canada.

Each year thousands of visitors make their way to the castle. They wander through the richly panelled entrance hall to the book-filled library. They drift through the double drawing room, a room designed for 'musical evenings' in which the $50,000 Steinway grand piano looks very much at home. They move on to the dining room with its huge oak sideboard, to the smoking room presided over by Sir Walter Raleigh enjoying a pipe in his stained glass window, and they climb the grand staircase, seventy-one steps to the fourth floor ballroom, and on another sixteen steps to the top of the castle's tower, a giddy sixty feet above the garden below and from where they can enjoy a view stretching more than twenty miles in all directions.

And no matter how helpful the guides, no matter how many questions are thoughtfully answered, Craigdarroch's visitors want to know more. They want to know more about the Dunsmuirs, the family for whom it was built; more about the architects who managed to produce a building which is at once magnificent and comfortable; and more about the castle's past — the eighteen years during which Craigdarroch housed British Columbia's richest family; its 'white elephant' years when no one knew quite what to do with it; its college years when students 'pitched a little woo' hidden away in its nooks and crannies; the years when the castle echoed with music and unimpressed ten-year-olds clattered up its stairs to pound away at a half-hour lesson on one of the thirty-five pianos which had appeared in the most unexpected places; and the years of the 'Second Battle of Craigdarroch' when a grumpy, rumpled curmudgeon emerged triumphant over bureaucratic disinterest.

Craigdarroch was written to satisfy the curiosity of those who have toured the castle, to whet the appetite of those who might be planning a visit, and to provide an 'armchair tour' for those who might never see the castle but who enjoy a stroll through the past.

A detailed room-by-room description of the castle has not been included. That information, up-dated as restoration continues, can be found in *A Guide to Craigdarroch* available at the castle or through Orca Books.

'Coal is King. And Dunsmuir is Coal'

Craigdarroch was built as the home of Robert Dunsmuir, the richest man in nineteenth century British Columbia. Dunsmuir had risen from near-poverty to become a capitalist icon, a coal-baron and railway-tycoon, a millionaire who had entered politics to make the province safe for his various enterprises and upon whom hundreds of British Columbians depended for their jobs.

To some he was a robber-baron, a man whose fortune was based on the niggardly wages he paid his employees and on the open-handed assistance he received from the government. To others he was a capitalist paragon, an altruist who worked hard and risked his own money to increase the wealth of the province rather than to line his own pockets.[1] For those who cast Dunsmuir in the role of hero, Craigdarroch was evidence of his generosity and selflessness; the castle, they argued, was built only to fulfill an old promise to a faithful wife. For others, Craigdarroch was nothing less than an example of monumental self-indulgence.

Robert Dunsmuir was born in Scotland in 1825 into a family whose livelihood had come from the coal beds of Ayrshire for at least three generations. When he was twenty-five, a young married man with two infant daughters, Dunsmuir made the most important decision of his life. He would leave the familiar Scottish mines and take his family on a ten thousand-mile voyage to the end of the earth, around Cape Horn to the north-east coast of 'Vancouver's Island' where he would work the unproven coal mines recently opened by the Hudson's Bay Company. For the four other colliers who made a similar choice and sailed from the Company's London docks in December 1850, that decision would end in disappointment and disillusionment, and as soon as their three-year contract with the Company expired, they would slip back to Scotland. But Dunsmuir remained behind and,

In this photograph, probably taken when he was in his late thirties, Robert Dunsmuir looks more like a timid bank clerk than a robber-baron. Before his death at the age of sixty-three he had found a better tailor and he had assumed an appearance of well cared for prosperity, but the strangely haunted look in his pale eyes remained and he retained the odd little under-the-chin beard which was perhaps intended to add strength to his jaw line.

whether through foresight or simply good fortune, he found himself the right man in the right place at the right time.

Dunsmuir's first years on the Island were spent at Fort Rupert, near present-day Port McNeill. Fort Rupert, a small collection of rough log buildings protected by a stockade and guarded by a bastion, stood near the beach, all but surrounded by an Indian encampment. The closest white settlement was Fort Victoria, on the southern tip of the Island and a 270-mile canoe trip away.

Wadham Nestor Diggle, Robert Dunsmuir's original partner, invested $10,000 in 'Dunsmuir & Diggle' in 1869 when he was a young naval lieutenant. He returned to England shortly after the death of his wife Emma in 1881. Two years later he sold his interests in the coal mines; the $600,000 he received allowed him to live in ease until his death in 1934.

² Diggle is described as the 'only son of the late Rev. Charles Diggle' in the *Colonist*, April 11, 1880. His age is given by J. K. Nesbitt, 'Admirals' Gold Helped Dig Dunsmuir Coalmines,' *Colonist*, Nov. 17, 1957.

Isolation, harassment by the Indians and lack of success in locating the coal beds which the Company had confidently predicted they would find, had a discouraging effect on the other miners, but while they grumbled and complained and counted the days until their contracts expired, Robert Dunsmuir concentrated on his work.

In the winter of 1852, the Hudson's Bay Company decided to move the colliers down the coast to Nanaimo, where it was hoped that the men would find the rich seams of coal that had eluded them at Fort Rupert. When his contract expired in 1854, Dunsmuir chose to remain at Nanaimo rather than return to Scotland with the other miners. But he did not sign a second contract that would have bound him to the HBC for a further three years. Instead, he suggested to the Company that he manage a coal seam. Rather than receiving a wage, he would sell to the Company the coal he raised. For the next fifteen years he continued to work in this way, managing the development of coal seams for the Hudson's Bay Company and the other companies that replaced it in the field. In 1869 when he discovered and acquired the rights to a previously unknown coal seam near Diver Lake, a few miles north of Nanaimo, he was the most experienced mine manager on the Island.

As well as expertise in opening and working Island coal beds, he had an intimate knowledge of the local market. What he lacked was the capital to develop his mines. Officers of the Royal Navy were only too happy to provide that commodity.

The Royal Navy had been on the scene since the mid 1850's, protecting the British Colony of Vancouver Island from potential Russian and American aggression. In 1865 a naval base had been established at Esquimalt, near Victoria on the southern tip of the Island, and the Navy's ships had become the best local customers of Vancouver Island coal. Naval officers, many of them from wealthy aristocratic families, remained alert to the possibilities of colonial investments. Some put their money into Cariboo gold mines, but the really smart investors opted for coal.

Dunsmuir's first partner was twenty-one year old Sub-Lieutenant Wadham Nestor Diggle of *HMS Boxer*.² The son of a clergyman, Diggle was not a wealthy man but from 1869 to 1871 he had managed to contribute, partly in time and partly in cash,

When they first went to Nanaimo in 1852, Robert and Joan Dunsmuir lived in one of the two-roomed log cabins built by the Hudson's Bay Company for its employees. The Dunsmuir's cabin stood on Front Street near the bastion. In this early sketch it may be one of the small buildings that can be seen partly obscured by the structures in the foreground.

an amount equivalent to $8000 to the partnership. In 1871, with their Wellington Colliery operational but needing expansion, Rear Admiral Arthur Farquhar was persuaded to invest $12,000 to become an equal partner.[3] Two years later the partnership was expanded to include Captain Frederick Wilbraham Egerton[4] who like Farquhar remained a silent partner, taking a quarter of the profits, but leaving the management of the mine to Dunsmuir and the responsibility for arranging coal sales to Diggle. Each of the original partners received a bonus of ten cents; Dunsmuir for every ton of coal he raised; Diggle for each ton he sold.

At first Diggle had handled sales in San Francisco, the most important coal market on the coast. But he was still in the navy and as the production of their colliery increased, the partners decided that a full-time American agent was required. They reached an agreement with San Franciscan Henry Berryman and the arrangement worked well until Berryman made the mistake of trying to cheat his Vancouver Island associates. In 1878 when

[3] Robert Dunsmuir, W. N. Diggle and Rear Admiral A. Farquhar — Articles of Partnership (G. Graham Collection, PABC) Total capitalization of Dunsmuir & Diggle was $32,000. Dunsmuir was judged to have already contributed in money and labour an amount equal to $10,000. Diggle was required to contribute an extra $2,000 to make his share equal to Dunsmuir's.

Dunsmuir & Diggle, Dissolution of Partnership, May 12, 1883 (Graham Collection, PABC)

he learned that Berryman was using Wellington coal as a security against personal indebtedness, Dunsmuir travelled to San Francisco, filed an injunction against Berryman's and 'successfully adjusted affairs' by taking over Berryman's business.[5] Dunsmuir had learned a lesson he would not soon forget — if you want something done right, do it yourself — and even as his commercial empire expanded, it remained tightly controlled by Robert and later by his sons, with the help of only a few individuals who could be implicitly trusted.

In 1879 Farquhar and Egerton sold their interests to Diggle and Dunsmuir. Diggle received his release from the navy and after a quick trip to England to collect a bride, he settled in San Francisco where he took over the sale of Wellington coal. In 1881 his wife Emma died. 'The previous day she had been perfectly well and had been out riding with her husband,' the *Colonist* reported.[6] A distraught Wadham Diggle accompanied her embalmed body back to England for burial and it seems that during that voyage he decided against returning to the West Coast. In 1883 he sold his share of the business to Dunsmuir. The $600,000 Diggle received brought him more than a fair return on his original investment and suggests, that since Diggle was an equal partner, Dunsmuir's Wellington Colliery was worth at least $1,200,000.[7]

By 1883 Dunsmuir, had he included only his coal mines, could have counted himself one of the richest men on the Pacific Coast, his only competition coming from San Franciscans, from men like Charles Crocker and Leland Stanford, whose vast fortunes had been founded on the lucrative subsidies they had received for constructing the Central Pacific Railroad and whose exuberantly extravagant mansions dominated San Francisco's Nob Hill. It would be in partnership with these men that Dunsmuir signed a contract with the Canadian government that raised him to truly multi-millionaire status.

In 1871 the Colony of British Columbia joined Confederation to become the fifth province of the Dominion of Canada. A condition of British Columbia's entry had been the construction of a transcontinental rail line which would link the Pacific coast with the Canadian provinces in the east. Using islands in the Gulf as stepping stones to Vancouver Island, the tracks were expected to end at Esquimalt. But when surveys indicated that seven spans,

[5] *Colonist*, October 4, 1878

[6] *Colonist*, June 9, 1881

[7] Dissolution of Partnership, May 12, 1883 (Graham Collection, PABC) It is difficult to assess the worth of nineteenth century dollars, but some comparison might be achieved by multiplying by a factor of ten. In other words Dunsmuir's Wellington Colliery would be worth at least $12,000,000 today.

six of them almost a quarter of a mile in length, would be required to bridge the Gulf, the federal government, recoiling in horror at the notion of adding an additional twenty million dollars to already astronomical construction costs, announced that the tracks would end at Vancouver; on the mainland rather than on Vancouver Island. With Islanders threatening open revolt, the Canadian Prime Minister, John A. Macdonald, who happened to sit in the federal house as a member for Victoria, searched for a compromise. The expense of having the tracks cross to the Island could not be tolerated; however the government might be persuaded to subsidize the construction of an Island railway which would link the communities of Esquimalt and Nanaimo, which would, in turn, be linked to the mainland terminus by a fleet of steamers.

Later, Dunsmuir apologists would suggest that he had seen the construction of the Island railway as a civic duty, that feelings of *noblesse oblige* had persuaded him to undertake the enterprise and that he had been 'induced' to become involved by the 'diplomatic pleadings' of Canada's Governor General, the Marquis of Lorne. As one biographer put it, 'It may be that this high official was finally instrumental in persuading Robert to commence the project . . . but one would prefer to think that it was his sense of responsibility to the people he represented and among whom he had become a name for stability, honesty and right dealing.'[8] Well, perhaps. But the opportunity to have the public finance a rail line that would connect his Wellington Colliery with Esquimalt, combined with the rich subsidies the government was prepared to offer, may have been incentive enough.

In 1882, the provincial government received two applications from consortiums seeking a charter to construct the Island railway. It accepted the application submitted by the 'Vancouver Land and Railway Company' headed by Lewis M. Clements. When Clements proved unable to raise the necessary capital, the government turned to the second applicant, Robert Dunsmuir, who had solved the problem of capital by forming a partnership with Crocker, Stanford and Huntington, the three surviving members of the Central Pacific's 'Big Four,' who, as well as having funds to invest, knew a thing or two about building railways and about winkling subsidies out of governments.

Forced to pass through rugged country, the E & N Railway was not the easiest line to build. This bridge near Goldstream was only one of many trestles required to span the deep canyons that lay along the route. That Dunsmuir completed the line ahead of schedule was a testament to his managerial abilities.

[8] James Audain, *From Coalmine to Castle* (New York: Pageant Press, 1955)

In a contract signed on August 12, 1883 Dunsmuir and his partners agreed to build the line in exchange for an outright subsidy of $750,000 to cover construction costs and a land grant of almost two million acres, a quarter of the total acreage of Vancouver Island.[9] Dunsmuir now stood unchallenged as the richest man in British Columbia.

'Fairview'

Even before the railway contract was finalized, Robert Dunsmuir had decided to shake the coal dust of Nanaimo from his shoulders. It wasn't as if Nanaimo hadn't made *some* progress since the 1850's when it had been characterized as the home of 'a few drunken miners and rowdy sailors.' After all by 1864 an enthusiast had been able to declare that it was 'well surveyed and dry.'[10] But even so, it had little to offer the province's richest man and by 1881 Dunsmuir was quietly making plans to live in a place and on a scale more appropriate to his status.

Like other servants of the Hudson's Bay Company, he had begun his Nanaimo years in one of the Company's small squared-log cabins which stood along Front Street near the Bastion overlooking the harbour. Recollections of early residents of Nanaimo offer confusing and conflicting evidence, but it seems likely that in 1858 Dunsmuir moved his family up the hill to a site that would become the corner of Albert and Wallace Streets when the town was properly surveyed. There he built a 'more commodious' residence.[11] The new house was a testament to Robert's expanding family rather than his expanding fortune, for by then Joan had given birth to six of their ten children and the house, standing in the sea of mud that passed for Nanaimo streets, was plain and unpretentious.[12]

In 1869, soon after opening the Wellington Colliery, Dunsmuir built a no-nonsense, twelve room, two-storey frame house on Jingle Pot Road near Diver Lake. He may have moved his family into this country house while 'Ardoon,' their new Nanaimo home, was being built.[13] With its gothic styling and gingerbread decorations, 'Ardoon' was one of the grandest houses in the coal town. By 1881 it was being tended by a staff of three — a Chinese

[9] Contract — Esquimalt-Nanaimo Railway, August 20, 1883 (PABC-VF)

[10] *The British Columbian*, August 13, 1864

[11] See Appendix One.

[12] Victor Harrison, cited *Nanaimo Retrospective* (Nanaimo: Nanaimo Historical Society, 1979)

[13] See Appendix One.

cook, an English housemaid and a Swedish gardener.[14] It was a home befitting a man who was now seen as 'at the hub of things' in Nanaimo but it would hardly do for a man who was worth as much as a million dollars.

Before he left with his family for a triumphal visit to his Ayrshire birthplace in the spring of 1882, Dunsmuir purchased five and a half acres of land in Victoria, the province's increasingly gracious capital city. The home of government and the center of power, Victoria was only three miles distant from the Esquimalt Naval Base. And thanks to the presence in the city of high-born, well-bred young naval officers, Victoria's society, led by the Lieutenant Governor and centered on Government House, positively glittered. To a man described as 'brusque,' 'practical'

Plain and practical, the twelve room house Robert Dunsmuir built in the countryside near his Wellington Colliery later became the home of the company doctor. In contrast, his Nanaimo home 'Ardoon' was more carefully designed and more attention was paid to its exterior decoration.

[14] Federal Census, 1881

Its grounds enclosed by a decorative fence, 'Ardoon' appears in the foreground almost hidden by trees. The little building that can be seen butted up against the main house may be the cabin Dunsmuir built for his family in 1857. Behind the trees is the stable in which Dunsmuir kept the fast horse and buggy which daily took him out to the mines.

and 'shrewd and capable,' the twitterings of society can have held little appeal. But Dunsmuir had a houseful of unmarried daughters, and the best husbands his money could buy were much more likely to be found in the capital city than in the mine-centered, working class town of Nanaimo.

Of the eight daughters Joan Dunsmuir bore her husband, only three were safely married by the time Robert decided to move to Victoria. Elizabeth and Agnes, born in Ayrshire before the family left for Vancouver Island, had married Nanaimo men — Elizabeth wedding mine manager John Bryden in 1867, and Agnes marrying shopkeeper James Harvey in 1870. Her father's increasing wealth and prominence attracted a suitor from farther afield to the third daughter, Marion. In 1879 she married Charles Frederick Houghton, the rancher from the Okanagan who had served in the federal parliament as the member for Yale and who in 1873 had become Deputy Adjutant-General in the Militia. In 1877, two years before he won Marion, Houghton and the militia he commanded had played a key role in smashing a miners' strike at Dunsmuir's colliery — an action that no doubt endeared him

Marion was one of three Dunsmuir daughters who had married before the family moved to Victoria and before her father had reached multi-millionaire status. She might have done better had she waited. The marriage was not an overwhelming success; Marion's coolness to her husband perhaps based on her discovery that he had left behind an Indian wife and children when he gave up his Okanagan ranch to take command of the militia.

to Marion's father.

For Mary Jane, Emily Ellen, Jessie Sophia, Annie Euphemia and Henrietta Maud, Robert's fortune stood a good chance of attracting husbands who enjoyed high social standings, perhaps even a titled gentleman, one of the aristocratic young Englishmen who were delivered to Victoria by the Navy or who drifted through the city collecting colonial experiences and, if at all possible, new-rich wives to support old impoverished estates.

In addition to social concerns, Dunsmuir's move was prompted by practical considerations. Until 1882 he had been content to exercise a behind-the-scenes influence on government policy, but with his sons having gained experience in operating and managing the mines, he decided to give them more responsibility while he became directly involved in politics by 'agreeing to accept nomination and election' as a member for Nanaimo in the next provincial election.

In December of 1882, the Victoria *Colonist* corrected a rumour that Robert Dunsmuir, who to no one's surprise had been successful in his quest for a parliamentary seat, was planning to lease 'Duval Cottage,' on Belcher Road near the Lieutenant Governor's house, for the duration of the parliamentary session.

'Mr. Dunsmuir will shortly proceed to the erection of a handsome family residence on Cadboro Bay road,' the *Colonist* informed its readers in an announcement that proved to be more than a little premature.[15] It was true enough that Dunsmuir had made the first in a series of purchases that would result in his control of the single most spectacular residential building site in the city, but by December of 1882 he was still almost twenty-three acres short of his goal and he had made plans to move his family into the more modest premises which would serve as his home for six years while he planned and built his dream-castle.

On September 26, 1884 he bought a house belonging to one of Victoria's wealthier residents, Captain Lewis Manville Starr.[16] An American, Starr had made a fortune by winning control of the steamboat traffic on Puget Sound. In 1878 Starr and his wife Eliza Jane paid $4000 to buy a 'commodious dwelling house, together with the two full-sized lots' at the corner of Quebec and Menzies Streets.[17] The two-storey frame house that stood on the property may have seemed 'commodious' to some, but not to Starr, who immediately announced that he intended to make 'extensive improvements.' The city's accessor took one look at Starr's large addition, which included a double-height bay window and a two-storey semi-tower topped with a coronet-like decoration, and decided that the value of the house had more than quadrupled.[18]

Within three years of completing his alterations, Starr removed to San Francisco. His decision to return to the United States coincided with the Dunsmuirs' decision to move to Victoria. Robert Dunsmuir may have been attracted to the Starr house because of its location, immediately across the street from the parliament buildings. But perhaps more importantly 'Fairview,'

[15] *Colonist*, December 5, 1882

[16] Register of Absolute Fees, vol. 8, fo. 85, (Land Registry, Victoria)

[17] *Colonist*, January 14, 1879

[18] Assessment Roll 1879-1880 (VCA)

During Captain Starr's tenancy, 'Fairview' (top) was surrounded by a humble fence and appeared raw and just-finished. Dunsmuir began living in the house in 1883. By 1884 he had acquired title to 'Fairview.' He purchased two adjacent lots and began to make the improvements that can be seen below which included a handsome stable and a noble stone and iron fence with an imposing corner entrance.

as the house was christened, was one of the most expensive residences in Victoria and it was spacious enough to serve as a setting for the lavish entertainments that the Dunsmuirs began to host after taking up residence in the city.

A fancy dress party held at 'Fairview' in December of 1885 was fulsomely described in the *Colonist* which devoted twenty-two column inches to detail the social event of the season.[19] Crowded into 'Fairview' were over one hundred guests including Sir Michael Culme-Seymour and several other 'gentlemen of the navy' resplendent in full dress uniform; two judges, a senator, and the mayor; and the cream of Victoria society, most of whom had obeyed instructions to appear in costume.

Nineteen year old Jessie Dunsmuir and her thirteen year old sister, Maud, were disguised as 'Italian peasant girls.' Emily Ellen, twenty-one and the oldest unmarried daughter, drifted about looking ethereally chilly in swansdown and frosted moss in a costume she described as 'Winter,' attracting admiring glances from a 'Turkish Pasha' who in ordinary life gloried in the name Northing Pinkney Snowden and whom Emily would marry at 'Fairview' six months later.

'The party was unanimously voted by the participants to be the pleasantest of the kind that has ever taken place in this province,' the *Colonist* reported with a contented sigh.

Victoria society was certainly prepared to accept the invitations tendered by a host and hostess renowned for open-handed hospitality, but even so the Dunsmuirs were regarded as not quite the thing; no matter how rich, they would never be seen as occupying the top drawer of Victorian society. The Dunsmuir daughters in particular were viewed with a kind of vague contempt based on their stolidity, their too often apparent bad humour and their tendency to overdress. As Kathleen O'Reilly, a friend of Jessie's, confided to her mother, 'I never see any people so much dressed as the Dunsmuirs. I don't think it is considered good taste . . .'[20]

During the winter season of 1886, Robert and Joan decided to hold a ball at the Assembly Hall on Government Street, a setting that allowed them to extend the guest list beyond the hundred that could be comfortably accommodated at 'Fairview.' A 'splendid supper' was served and dancing to the music of Professor Haynes' orchestra kept up until an early hour. 'There were a large number of the *elite* present and full evening dress was quite the thing,' the *Victoria Times* rhapsodized.[21]

The Dunsmuirs' ball was not, however, deemed to be *the* social event of the season. That honour went to the ball given two weeks later by seventy-nine year old Lady Douglas, the half-breed widow of fur-trader Sir James Douglas.[22] Born in Demerara, the son of a Scots plantation manager and a 'free coloured woman,' Douglas had been knighted by Queen Victoria for his services as the first governor of British Columbia. Lady Douglas' title, her status as the Governor's widow and her position as one of Victoria's earliest residents, combined with the income she received from the one thousand acre Fairfield Estate that had formed part of Sir James' bequest to his family, gave Amelia Douglas pride of place in Victoria's society.

The Dunsmuirs certainly enjoyed all the status that money could buy, but there was a feeling in Victoria that they spent ostentatiously rather than well. Craigdarroch, the house that served as Dunsmuir's monument to his success would be seen by some as yet another example of the family's tendency to spend conspicuously without getting value for money.

Dream Castles

A legend has attached itself to the building of Craigdarroch. Robert, the story goes, promised his wife Joan that he would build her a castle if she agreed to leave Scotland and accompany him to Vancouver Island. Accordingly, he acquired twenty-eight of the highest, most prominent acres in the city and he built the most expensive residence in the province not as an expression of self-importance but simply to fulfill a thirty-five year old promise. To Dunsmuir supporters the appeal of this version of events is clear for it tends to ennoble and romanticize the lavish personal expenditures of a man who had a reputation for being hard-nosed and tight-fisted when dealing with the men who worked his mines.

Whatever its original source — whether it was begun by Dunsmuir himself or whether it was put about after his death to counteract suggestions that he was an unscrupulous robber-baron

[21] *Victoria Times*, January 14, 1887
[22] *Victoria Times*, January 29, 1887

Determination is written all over Joan Dunsmuir's square-jawed, thin-lipped little face. She was sensible and practical and an astute advisor to her husband.

[23] *Colonist*, October 3, 1908

[24] *Colonist*, May 16, 1877

[25] Willis Polk cited by Oscar Lewis, *The Big Four*, (New York: Alfred A. Knopf, 1959)

[26] Sanders is often identified as Saunders, but since his drawings were signed 'Sanders' and the firm's advertisements (see for example, *New Westminster Times*, February 13, 1861) used the same spelling it might be safe to conclude that 'Sanders' is correct.

who chose to live in luxury while men died in his mines — the story would seem to be the product of wishful fantasy rather than fact.

One glance at Joan Dunsmuir — a pause to appreciate the character that projects from that thin-lipped, square-jawed little face — is enough to suggest that she would not have been persuaded by so romantic a promise, especially one that her husband would, in 1850, have seemed so unlikely to be able to fulfill. Furthermore, those who knew both Joan and Robert well insist that she was more equal business partner than subservient helpmate. 'It is said that more than once Mrs. Dunsmuir saved the situation and by her great force of character, and with her resourceful brain, solved the problem that looked like destruction to the vast estate which Mr. and Mrs. Dunsmuir accumulated,' an associate recalled.[23]

So it seems more likely that Robert, a delicately-featured little man who appears the shortest in any male group, built Craigdarroch for himself, as a symbol of his power and wealth. And if Dunsmuir chose his house to serve as his monument, he was simply following the examples set by the members of the 'Big Four,' the San Franciscans who were his partners in the Esquimalt and Nanaimo Railroad.

During the 1870's the California railway tycoons had scrambled to outdo each other, competing for the best building sites atop San Francisco's Nob Hill and then endeavouring to build houses of uniquely eyestopping extravagance and grandeur. One of the hill-top palaces was estimated to have cost three million dollars.[24] As one architectural critic wrote in the 1880's, 'They cost a great deal of money and whatever harsh criticism may fall upon them, they cannot be robbed of that prestige.'[25]

Mark Hopkins, the only member of the 'Big Four' who died before he had a chance to do business with Dunsmuir, appears to have won the 'house as monument' battle. Designed by architects Wright and Sanders,[26] the huge house straddled the hill and while it might best be described as gothic, it seems to have attempted to combine elements of every architectural style known to man. Adorned with a dizzying array of round towers and steeply-pitched roofs and boasting a three-storey, domed conservatory, the mansion was dominated by a fifty-foot-high square

The mansions of San Francisco's Bonanza Kings provided examples of the scale of investment appropriate to millionaire housebuilders. Seeming to be a combination of every architectural style known to man, Mark Hopkins' Nob Hill mansion (top) was rumoured to have cost as much as three million dollars. Charles Crocker's residence (bottom) described as 'a delirium of the wood carver' stood higher on the hill than its nearest neighbour, the understated Italianate house belonging to fellow millionaire David Colton. The odd looking structure which appears to be between the two houses is Crocker's 'spite fence' which enclosed the property of a local undertaker who had refused to sell.

tower which was itself ornamented with a church-like steeple. After entering through a structure resembling a castle gatehouse, guests to the house feasted their eyes on a drawing room modeled on a room found in the Palace of the Doges; on a dining room, panelled to the ceiling in carved English oak and large enough to seat sixty people; on a master bedroom finished with ivory-inlaid ebony; and on a library 'so beautiful that only poetry should be read there.'[27]

But perhaps the most important features of the Hopkins' mansion were its siting and its bulk, both of which allowed it to loom pretentiously over its nearest neighbour which just happened to belong to fellow 'Big Four' member, Leland Stanford. Compared to the Hopkins' house, Stanford's residence gave the impression of being positively understated, despite such touches as the 'little embroidered ruching modestly flouncing the third story windows.'[28]

As Charles Crocker ably demonstrated, it was more than the view that had encouraged him and his partners to build on the hill. Ignoring the folly of 'cutting off one's nose to spite one's face,' Crocker was so irritated after one recalcitrant land owner refused to sell and thus prevented him from acquiring an entire city block, that he built an enormous wooden 'spite fence' some thirty feet high which surrounded the man's property but also effectively cut off Crocker's own views from the house that had cost as much as one and a quarter million dollars to build.

In Victoria Dunsmuir had selected the site for the mansion he would build even before he moved to the city. By February of 1882 he had spent $4,200 to buy five and a half acres along Fort Street.[29] He had to wait until October of 1885 before he was able to secure a key piece of property — the eight and a half acres that included the ideal site for the construction of his house. He would continue to add to his holdings until by 1888 he had acquired just over twenty-eight acres, but by 1885 he was certainly ready to begin thinking about the plans for his residence. If he faced any problem, it was Victoria's lack of an architect with experience in building the scale of house needed to satisfy his ambition.

In 1885, the city was home to only eight architects, and not all of them regarded architecture as a full time profession.[30] The

[27] Lewis, *Big Four*

[28] Polk, *Big Four*

[29] K.M. Keddy and B. W. Davies, History in Art, undergraduate paper (CCA)

[30] The Victoria City Business Directory (Williams) 1884/1885 lists S. C. Burris, Harris & Hargreaves, H. H. Leslie, E. Mallandaine, John Teague, H. O. Tiedemann and Thomas Trounce. Besides Teague only Burris seems to have found enough work to support himself as an architect. (see for example *Times,* December 31, 1887)

busiest was John Teague. During 1885, he designed more than twenty buildings, including the Archbishop's Palace on Yates Street which was acknowledged to be 'the most substantial, the handsomest and the costliest' residence built in the city over the year.[31]

In 1886 Teague would again be credited with the design of the year's most expensive residence. Built for James Allan Grahame, 'Allandale' was a three-storey wooden structure with large bay windows, verandahs, balconies, a conservatory, a billiard room and an entrance hall panelled in antique oak, mahogany and maple. It was judged to be 'one of the most artistic homes in the city.'[32] But even so, 'Allandale,' like the Archbishop's Palace, had cost only $25,000 to build. According to the lowest estimate, Dunsmuir planned to spend at least six times that much on Craigdarroch and he might be forgiven if he felt that the construction of his castle was beyond the expertise of Teague or any other Victoria architect.[33]

Dunsmuir may have toyed with the idea of using a San Francisco architect. But perhaps not, for much closer to home, in Portland, Oregon, there was a man with a proven reputation, who was familiar with Victoria and with whose work Dunsmuir may well have been intimately acquainted.

Warren Heywood Williams was born in 1844 in New York City.[34] In 1849 his architect father, Stephen Hedders Williams, heard about the gold discoveries along California's Sacramento River and decided to move his family to the booming gold-mad city of San Francisco, where, he guessed correctly, opportunities for an ambitious architect would be unsurpassed. Early in the 1860's Williams invited his son to join the firm as a draftsman. Warren Williams had been elevated to partner and the firm rechristened 'Stephen H. Williams & Son' by 1869, when he was sent to Portland to supervise the construction of the new Odd Fellows Temple, then the tallest building in Portland and described in the city's 1870 Directory as 'one of the finest buildings in Portland and an ornament to the city.'

Like his father, Williams remained alert to golden opportunities and when he learned in December, 1872 that a fire had devastated much of downtown Portland he decided to leave his father's practice and move to the Oregon city to take advantage of the

Warren Heywood Williams was Portland's busiest architect. He died in 1888 two years before Craigdarroch, his most important residential commission, was completed.

[31] *Colonist,* January 1, 1886

[32] *Times,* December 31, 1887

[33] It has been suggested that Dunsmuir based his choice of an architect on his desire to keep details of his house secret, but it seems more likely that he simply wanted to select a man who he felt confident could complete the job satisfactorily.

[34] W. J. Hawkins III, 'Warren Heywood Williams, Architect (1844-1888),' *Portland Friends of Cast-Iron Architecture Newsletter,* December, 1980

Designed by Warren Williams and completed in 1885, the Victoria branch of the Bank of British Columbia, with its extensive use of applied cast-iron decoration, set a new standard for buildings in the city's commercial district.

reconstruction building boom. A second fire, in August of 1873, destroyed twenty business blocks along the river and Williams was commissioned to replace many of them.

Working sometimes with a partner and sometimes alone, Williams became the city's busiest and most prominent architect. In the business district, he was responsible for dozens of trend-setting commercial buildings, including the Labbes' Block, built in 1880 and the first full four-storeyed block in the city.

It was Williams' reputation for producing grand and impressive commercial structures that suggested to the Bank of British Columbia that he would be the best man to design its new Victoria headquarters, to be located at the corner of Government and Fort Streets, the city's most important intersection. In October, 1884 the bank announced that its new offices would cost some $50,000 and would be 'erected immediately.'[35] On March 13, 1885 Williams arrived in the city and revealed his plans for the most

[35] *Colonist,* October 14, 1884

ornate bank building Victoria would ever see. In a city whose plain, brick commercial buildings had been characterized as 'good, heavy and substantial,' the new Bank of B. C. appeared arrestingly fanciful and quite beautiful. It was, according to the *Colonist*, 'the most perfect piece of architecture so far existing in this province.'[36]

Even if Williams' practice had been limited to commercial buildings, Dunsmuir's choice of the Portlander as his architect would have been understandable, but Williams was also responsible for some of Portland's most imposing mansions. In 1874, shortly after he took up residence in the city, he had designed an elegant house for Henry W. Corbett, the city's wealthiest citizen. And during the 1880's his houses, dotted here and there throughout the city's most distinguished neighbourhood, led people to make favourable comparisons between Portland's Nineteenth Street and San Francisco's Nob Hill.

But Dunsmuir may have had an even more compelling reason for selecting Williams as his architect. It is highly likely that Williams had designed the Dunsmuir home 'Fairview.' Its scale and styling were very similar to Williams' Portland houses. The Morris Marks house, in particular, bore a striking resemblance to 'Fairview.' And there was certainly a connection between Williams and Captain Starr, the builder of 'Fairview.' Before coming to Victoria, Starr had lived in Portland where he had been known as 'one of the most prominent capitalists and bankers in the city' and where he owned several large parcels of commercial property. Starr would have followed Williams' career with interest as the architect re-shaped the city's commercial core and its best residential district. And it is reasonable to speculate that Starr decided to commission the Portland architect to design the large addition to his Victoria home. If he did, then Dunsmuir had been living in a Williams-designed house for over a year when he commissioned the architect to prepare plans for Craigdarroch.

Sometime in 1885 when Williams was in Victoria to check on the progress of his bank building, Dunsmuir must have led him out along Fort Street, up the hill, through glades of oak trees and over moss-covered stones, to the rocky prominence he had selected for his house. Turning to survey the view — the city and the Sooke Hills to the west, Mount Douglas to the north, sea

[36] *Colonist,* January 1, 1886

Designed by Warren Williams and built in Portland in 1882, the Morris Marks house bears a distinct resemblance to the Dunsmuir residence 'Fairview' constructed in Victoria three years earlier for former Portlander Captain Manville Starr.

glimpses to the east, and to the south the shimmering waters of the Strait of Juan de Fuca and the panorama of the snow-capped heights of the Olympic Range — Williams must have been impressed. And he must also have been impressed by the plans of his new client, for while Dunsmuir's precise instructions to his architect remain unknown, it might be safely concluded that they included the words 'spare no expense.'

A Proud Scot

Returning to Portland, Williams began working on the plans for the most ambitious residence he would ever design. His forte was the Italianate style which he used for both residences and commercial blocks; his foray into Scottish Baronial must have been an attempt to please his client, for Robert Dunsmuir was nothing if not a proud Scot.

A member of the Caledonian Society and the master of ceremonies at celebrations honouring the birth of Robert Burns, he was happy to boast that he and his wife Joan had grown up in Burns country and that they had attended school in Kilmarnock, the city in which the poet's works had first been published. When he christened his house 'Craigdarroch' he may have been thinking of the birthplace of Annie Laurie, the subject of one of Scotland's best known songs. But while Dunsmuir named his house 'Craigdarroch' and his architect produced a romantic Scottish fantasy that combined a variety of other architectural styles, to Victorians, who knew a castle when they saw one, the house was known simply as 'Dunsmuir Castle.'

If Dunsmuir did ask Williams to build him a castle, he would have been acting in a fine Victoria tradition. The Lieutenant Governor was housed in 'Cary Castle,' the former home of Vancouver Island's first Attorney General, George Hunter Cary. Eccentric to the point of madness, Cary had built his castle in the early 1860's when his investments in the Cariboo's 'Never Sweat' gold mine had begun to pay off. Designed by Fred Walter Green, who later found his true calling as a city engineer, Cary's castle had been described as 'a queer architectural intrusion on the wild landscape.' And queer it certainly was, for Cary's mine had not produced the expected returns and he had been forced to call a halt to construction before the building was completed. In 1866, the castle, including only a tower, topped with battlement-like crenellations, and a squat one storey wing which featured a most unlikely bay window, had been purchased by a newly-arrived Governor and had become by default, rather than by design, Government House.

Attempts by other Victorians to build castles were not always successful. 'Cary Castle' (top) was built in the early 1860's and was acknowledged to be one of Victoria's uglier buildings, a status it continued to enjoy until it became British Columbia's official Government House and public money was spent improving it by concealing as much of the original building as possible. Built during the 1870's, 'Armdale' (bottom) was another attempt to introduce elements of a remembered Old World castle to the raw newness of the west coast. But while it may have been a more successful exercise in nostalgia than 'Cary Castle,' 'Armdale' was not particularly pleasing as a work of architecture.

William Macdonald was another castle-builder whose efforts may have inspired Dunsmuir. Born on the Isle of Skye, Macdonald had arrived on Vancouver Island in 1851. Appointed to the Senate after British Columbia entered Confederation, Macdonald was a wealthy man, his fortune founded on shrewd property investments. In 1876 he began to build a large house on his land holdings in the James Bay neighbourhood. Christened 'Armadale' after Armadale Castle on the Isle of Skye, seat of the chief of the clan Macdonald, his home was an awkward combination of crenellated castle elements, including a square gatehouse and at least one fat round tower.

Unlike 'Cary Castle' and 'Armadale,' Craigdarroch would not be an attempt to replicate features of a remembered castle. Instead it would be an eclectic design, which combined a variety of architectural styles to create an impression, to produce a fairy tale castle rather than an accurate reproduction. Craigdarroch's castle-like aura was the result of its siting rather than its design. Historically castles had been built as fortified residences, protected by their encircling walls or by their impregnable locations. And like a laird's castle in a medieval hill town, Craigdarroch dominated Victoria's sky line.

By the summer of 1887, Williams' plans, at least for the castle's exterior, must have been complete; the contract for Craigdarroch's foundation was signed on September 20th of that year.[37] The lucky contractors were Thomas Moffat, a Scottish-born house builder and contractor, and John Mortimer, a stone mason and 'one of the most accomplished sculptors on the coast,' who had arrived in Victoria from Tacoma in 1878 and whose granite and marble works was located on Government Street near the James Bay bridge.[38]

Less than four months after its construction began, Craigdarroch's architect was dead. Warren Williams had been in failing health for some time. It may be that he realized his time was short, for in the winter of 1887 he was overcome by a desire to visit seldom-seen relatives in New York. Soon after arriving in that city in November he caught a severe cold and deciding that only the sunnier climes of California would result in a cure, he returned to the west coast. He died in Fresno on January 7, 1888 of 'an enlargement of the heart and other complications,' just a month

[37] Hugh Campbell, Diary, (CCA)

[38] Campbell records Mortimer and Moffat as contractors and their role is confirmed *Victoria Times,* December 31, 1887

Killyleagh Castle in County Down, Ireland is a good example of the Scottish Baronial style, typified by small round towers and designed to take advantage of craggy sites.

short of his 44th birthday.[39]

With Williams' death, responsibility for Craigdarroch slipped to Arthur Smith. Smith had been working as a draftsman in Williams' office since 1880 and in 1887, with Williams planning to be absent from the practice for some months, he had been elevated to the position of architect.[40] Because of the unusual way in which Williams organized his office, Smith should have been quite capable of bringing Craigdarroch to a successful completion.

[39] *The Sunday Oregonian,* January 8, 1888

[40] In Portland's 1880 Directory, Smith is listed as a draftsman residing in the same building in which Williams had his office. Smith is recorded as having worked as Williams' partner on only one other building, Temple Beth Israel, built in Portland in 1888, the year of Williams' death. (Watkins, *Newsletter*)

In 1882 Victoria architect Edward Mallandaine had been in Portland looking for work. So impressed had he been with Williams' unique 'system' and with his annual income of $40,000 that he had recorded his impressions in his memoirs.[41]

> I believe his method was in receiving an order, especially for a largish job, a church or a brick block, to hand it over to design to an assistant with general approval by himself. When all was ready for the contractor, the work was placed under the control of the draughtsman who designed it with general supervision by Mr Williams. The work and responsibility thus divided, more interest was naturally felt by each one for his part, and no doubt remuneration followed in proportion. It seems almost the only way to get thro much work. The reputation of the head of the office brings the work, he is responsible at first hand. Talent being secured in the subordinates, and it can always be had, by offering conmensurate(sic)pay, interest. . . is aroused and business efficiently carried on.

Smith's experience must have been much broader than might ordinarily be expected in a recently jumped-up draftsman, but now, without Williams' supervision, he may have been overwhelmed by the myriad details of the castle's interior finishing. His problems were compounded by a shortage of qualified workmen and later by the lack of interest with which the Dunsmuirs came to regard the castle.

Stonemasons were in such short supply that getting a job at the castle proved an easy task. The story of his hiring became one of Moses McGregor's favourite reminiscences and there is much to suggest that his experience was fairly typical.[42] Born in Belfast in 1851, McGregor was a trained stonemason and bricklayer when he arrived in Victoria in 1888. After his ship tied up at the foot of Yates, he wandered along Wharf Street and into the first hotel he found. Was there a chance, he asked the hotelkeeper, of a stonemason finding a job in Victoria?

'Yes, there might be,' the hotelman answered. 'There's a man here from 'Frisco who has been given a contract to build a castle for the Dunsmuirs.'[43]

[41] Edward Mallandaine, Reminiscences (PABC)

[42] F. M. McGregor to L. J. Wallace, October 3, 1966 (PABC-VF)

[43] A San Franciscan may well have served as Craigdarroch's general contractor. Although the name of local contractor Thomas Catteral has been connected with the castle, that connection seems to have been based on an article (Colonist, April 5, 1896) which lists Catteral's more important projects but while the list includes two Dunsmuir family houses, for James Dunsmuir and for Northing Pinkney Snowden, Craigdarroch does not appear.

The earliest known representation of Craigdarroch, this sketch appeared in 1889 in *The West Shore*, an illustrated magazine published in Portland. The architects are described as 'Williams and Smith,' Smith having chosen to claim co-authorship of the building after Williams' death the year before.

'There's a stranger coming up the street now — this may be the man.'

McGregor hurried outside, stopped the man, asked for a job and was hired on the spot. He would later recall that work on Craigdarroch was forced to cease for a time when no bricklayers could be found to work on the interior brickwork.

By all accounts, Craigdarroch was an extremely expensive building; Dunsmuir may have spent as much as half a million dollars to realize his dream and even if the castle cost less than half that much, it was still in a class by itself.[44] For the amount he spent, Dunsmuir had every right to expect perfection. That he didn't get it, must be due, at least in part, to Smith's lack of expertise. After proudly claiming co-authorship of Craigdarroch, he slid into anonymity, apparently never again working on any building of a similar scale or importance.

But Smith's inexperience alone cannot account for the oddly incomplete way in which the castle was finished; no architectural training was necessary to notice that a dining room door opened, not onto a verandah, a porch or a conservatory, but onto a four-foot drop. By far the most important factor must have

[44] see Appendix Two.

been the Dunsmuirs' changing attitude toward the building. The completion of the castle became a nagging obligation rather than an exciting project when, a year before Craigdarroch was ready for occupancy, Robert Dunsmuir died.

King Grab

On Saturday April 6, 1889 Robert Dunsmuir took to his bed with a severe cold. He was sixty-three years old and, other than being tired after the parliamentary session, he was thought to be in robust health. On April 10th he took a turn for the worse, lapsing into an unexplained coma. Efforts to revive him succeeded and his doctors were confidently predicting a full recovery when, on April 12th, he suffered a relapse. He rallied only briefly, awakening to find the Reverend Mr. McLeod bending over him. After mumbling a few fervent prayers on his own behalf, Dunsmuir lost consciousness. An hour later he was dead.

Obituary-writers for British Columbia newspapers pulled out all the stops. The *Victoria Daily Colonist*, whose editor enjoyed convivial business and personal relationships with the deceased, edged every column of every page in black, and delivered itself of a eulogy which ended in a call for a public funeral.

'He was regarded as the Province's chief and truest friend,' the *Colonist* keened. 'Every British Columbian today feels that he has lost a friend.'[45]

The *Colonist's* competitor, the *Victoria Times*, found itself in the appalling position of having recently criticized the man who now seemed destined for canonization as a capitalist saint. 'It was the misfortune of The *Times*, rather than its fault, that differences arose between it and Mr Dunsmuir, and sometimes these differences were of an acrimonious nature,' the editor blushed.[46]

Unlike the *Colonist* which seemed to operate under the assumption that Dunsmuir could do no wrong, the *Times* was often critical of the government asistance he received, in particular the subsidies that had accompanied the E & N railway contract. Witnessing the tumultuous reception that had greeted the arrival of the first E & N train to cross the Johnson Street bridge into

[45] *Colonist,* April 13, 1889

[46] *Times,* April 13, 1889

Robert Dunsmuir was the most popular man in Victoria on March 28, 1888 when the first E & N train steamed into the city. This arch (top), made of evergreens tied to a frame and featuring a portrait of Robert Dunsmuir at its peak, was built to celebrate the day. A sign attached to the arch reads 'Long Looked For. Come at Last.' Crowds gathered on Store Street (bottom) to cheer Dunsmuir's private railway car as it arrived at the station. 'Dunsmuir and More of 'Em,' reads the sign posted on the station and that sentiment was echoed by the majority of Victoria's citizens.

downtown Victoria, the editor of the *Times* had composed a telling indictment of Dunsmuir's policies. Written in 1888 a year before Dunsmuir's death and set to the tune of 'God Save The Queen,' it had suggested that Dunsmuir might spend eternity in someplace other than heaven.[47]

'Provincial Anthem'

I am King Grab, you see,
I own this country —
    I am King Grab
Now my bridge is complete,
Mayor, Councillors en fete
Come grovel at my feet,
    I am King Grab.

And when I come to die
You need not wail or cry:
    Yourselves console
Know that I am to be
Throughout eternity
Where there's no scarcity
    Or want of coal.

Now, the *Times* fell over itself trying to make amends. 'That Mr. Dunsmuir was other than a clear-headed, enterprising man, liberal-handed, amenable to reason, we never doubted,' the *Times* apologized.[48]

No one, it seems, was prepared to examine contrary opinions held by some of the men who laboured in Dunsmuir's coal pits and whose loathing for their employer was so deep that it became an article of family faith and so strong that even today a visit to Craigdarroch is regarded as a disloyal act by their descendants.

Dunsmuir was notorious for his opposition to any attempts by his miners to unionize and for his willingness to employ Chinese labourers who were prepared to accept lower wages and whose presence in the mines was said to constitute a safety hazard.

His handling of a strike in 1877 had ably demonstrated that he was prepared to take whatever means were necessary to discourage his miners from taking collective action to improve their lot. The trouble had begun a year earlier, in 1876, when

[47] *Times*, April 4, 1888
[48] *Times*, April 13, 1889

By the late 1880's Robert Dunsmuir appeared the very model of a millionaire capitalist. Here the heavy practical tweeds he favoured in earlier years have been replaced by a finely-tailored jacket complimented by a dotted velvet vest.

Dunsmuir announced that coal sales had fallen off, that the company had thousands of tons of unsold coal on its hands, and that if the men wished to continue working, they would have to accept a cut in pay. Rather than the $1.20 per ton he had been paying, he was forthwith reducing their wages to one dollar per ton. When sales improved, he would return them to the higher rate.

Reluctantly, but trusting Dunsmuir to be as good as his word, the men continued working. But the following year, with coal sales having increased and the company's storage bins near empty, they approached Dunsmuir and suggested that now might be the time to return to the old rate. Dunsmuir refused. The miners responded by laying down tools. When he discovered that over one hundred men, almost half of his work-force, were prepared to defy him, he decided that the time had come not only to settle this strike, but also to discourage future insurrections.

'Such a lot of men I never had to deal with before, and there will be no peace with them until they get a proper lesson,' he wrote.[49]

Dunsmuir launched a two-pronged attack. He hired strike-breakers, recruited in waterfront bars and saloons in San Francisco. And he evicted the colliers and their families from the company-owned cottages in which they lived.

'We are going to have trouble, if not bloodshed, when we attempt to evict the miners from the houses,' Dunsmuir predicted.[50]

Convinced that violence would erupt and appalled at the prospect of Dunsmuir acting on his threat to close down the mines for twelve months if the trouble continued, the government agreed to dispatch the militia. In theory, Lieutenant-Colonel Houghton and the 107 officers and men under his command, were protecting the Sheriff as he completed the process of physically removing the miners from their homes; but in reality they were protecting Dunsmuir's company and its ability to make the highest possible profits. With armed militiamen ready to interpret any resistance in the worst possible light and with a naval gun-boat standing by ready to provide assistance, the strikers gave up. With the exception of the five men who were charged with 'obstructing with violence,' and the seventy-five men who Dunsmuir refused to re-hire, they returned to work.

'The sudden collapse of the strike proves that the remuneration was ample,' the *Colonist* editorialized.[51]

The employment of Chinese in the mines was the basis of continuing complaints from the miners. Willing to work for half the pay of white miners, the Chinese, who had arrived in British Columbia in the thousands during the 1880's, were recognized by mine-managers as 'a weapon with which to settle disputes.'[52] By 1884 Dunsmuir was employing almost eight hundred Chinese and finding them to be excellent workers, he dismissed categorically any suggestion that their lack of mining experience and their inability to read posted warnings and regulations made them a danger to themselves and to the white miners who joined them underground at the pit face. But when in 1888 a violent explosion collapsed the east slope of the company's Number 5 pit, kill-

The miners' strike of 1877 was put down with the help of the militia commanded by Lieutenant-Colonel Houghton. Two years later Houghton married Dunsmuir's daughter Marion.

[49] R. Dunsmuir to Attorney-General, February 27, 1877, 'Correspondence-Wellington Strike,' *Sessional Papers,* 1878

[50] R. Dunsmuir to Attorney-General, February 25, 1877, *Sessional Papers,* 1878

[51] *Colonist,* June 6, 1877

[52] S. M. Robbins, cited James Morton, *In the Sea of Sterile Mountains* (Vancouver: J.J. Douglas, 1974)

ing thirty-one whites and forty-six Chinese, there were some who suggested that Dunsmuir was more interested in profits than in the safety of his men.

Robert Dunsmuir's sudden death crushed any enthusiasm Joan may have had for Craigdarroch. With the castle still abuilding and with decisions yet to be made regarding the grounds and the interior finishing, Joan, accompanied by two of her unmarried daughters, left Victoria for an extended tour of Europe which would include a visit to her family in Scotland. With Joan abroad, the melancholy job of completing the castle was left to her sons.

Doing it Right

James Dunsmuir was thirty-eight years old and his brother Alex was thirty-six when their father died. Both were regarded as hard, practical businessmen and neither was known for his artistic sensibilities. If the evidence of Craigdarroch's landscape gardener, Hugh Campbell, is to be believed, they approached the work still to be done on the castle with the same pragmatism, the same abrupt common sense, that characterized their business dealings.

Campbell and his sons arrived in Victoria from Glasgow on June 18, 1889. 'The day after we arrived in Victoria, I was told that a Mr. Dunsmuir was building a palatial residence here,' Hugh reported.[53] Before he approached the Dunsmuirs for a job, he walked out along Fort Street to survey the project.

"I went and had a look at it and eighteen acres of ground attached,' Campbell wrote. 'It is covered with a few large and good many small oak trees and at least ½ the ground is taken up with patches of rock, some on the surface and others 10 feet above it.'

Campbell decided to call at the Dunsmuir offices, where he spoke to one of the boys — probably James, the more cautious of the two brothers. 'I went to him, made enquiries, was told to prepare a plan of laying out the terraces, drives, gardens, stables, etc. so that it might be sent to Scotland for his widowed mother's approval.'

He spent a week preparing sketches and then returned to the Dunsmuirs' offices; this time he dealt with Alex. 'I presented my

[53] Hugh Campbell, Diary (CCA)

plan with all the strength I could muster . . . There and then he arranged I was to meet him on the grounds in two hours.'

Chronically impatient, Alex was anxious to see the work begin. He asked Campbell what kind of tools and how many men he required and told him to report to the site at seven the following Monday morning. Campbell may not have realized it at the time, but he had just been handed the largest private landscape contract in the city. That James and Alex had apparently given little thought to the gardens until approached by Campbell would seem to suggest that the family had come to view the castle as a burden, as something that had to be completed simply because it had been begun.

When Campbell arrived at the appointed time, he found tools and five Chinese labourers waiting for him. Soon he was joined by 'five more Chinamen and nine quarrymen, seven wagons (each

When Alexander Dunsmuir hired Hugh Campbell to lay out the estate, he may not have acquired the services of the most talented landscape gardener in town. Even considering that they appeared to best advantage when viewed from above, the shaped flower beds that can be seen in this early photograph do tend to look like randomly placed, inartistic clumps.

Included in the five railcars of hardwood finishing shipped from Chicago for the Dunsmuir residence was the golden oak panelling that lines the main hall and the staircase. It can be glimpsed, but not really appreciated, in this photograph taken during 'Christmas at Craigdarroch' celebrations in 1986.

54 *Victoria Times,* January 28, 1890. On July 24, 1890 the *Colonist* reported that five railway cars of hardwood finishing had recently been shipped from Chicago.

a pair of horses) and drivers' and by the middle of August the workforce had grown to twenty-three. Campbell, who sometimes had trouble getting his Scots tongue around Chinese names, recorded nine members of his team as Jim Chin, Lane Chin, One Eye, Black Spot, Sick Paw, Good Nat, Lady Kill, Long Fellow and Fie Hot.

Through the summer, winter and the following spring, Campbell and his team laboured to meet the deadline set by Alex. Work was to be finished by August 15, 1890. For each day after that, Campbell would be charged a penalty of five dollars. During the year he worked on the grounds, laying out terraces and building retaining walls and artificial lakes, Campbell seems to have been virtually unsupervised; his only instructions had been delivered by Alex and had been direct and simple. As Campbell confided to his diary, 'Our orders are to do it as we think best, and as economical as possible, but *do it right.*'

The August completion date set by Alex coincided with his timetable for the work on the castle's interior; it too was to be completed and ready for his mother's occupancy by the summer of 1890. In January, 1890 a contract was let for the interior woodwork; all the windows, doors, mouldings and panelling were to be made of 'choice and expensive woods.'[54] Bids had ranged from $30,000 to $45,000 and given that Alex had instructed his gardener to be 'as economical as possible,' it might be presumed that the Chicago firm of A.H. Andrews who won the contract had submitted the lowest bid.

Even if Alex did accept the lowest bid that would still have been consistent with his determination to do it right, for in 1890, $30,000 was an enormous amount to spend on a building's interior finishing. During 1890 Victoria experienced something of a construction boom; four hundred homes were completed before the year was out. Not one of those four hundred homes cost as much as the woodwork for Craigdarroch.

In May of 1890, Alex went to England to collect his mother and it seems likely that Joan moved into Craigdarroch sometime after her return to Victoria that summer. It would be a sad beginning for the house Robert Dunsmuir had intended as his monument. Joan had been in Switzerland when the news reached her that her second daughter, forty year old Agnes, had died of

In the only know photograph of the castle's interior taken during the Dunsmuirs' tenancy, Joan's granddaughter Elizabeth Harvey sits slightly apart from her aunts (from l to r.) Maud, Annie Euphemia and Jesse, as they pose for an afternoon of music and reading in the drawing room. At their feet is one of the three bearskin rugs that were to be found in the room. The rearing horse atop its marble pedestal was considered the *piece-de-resistance* of the Dunsmuir art collection.

typhoid during the epidemic that had swept Nanaimo in September of 1889.[55] In March of the following year, Agnes' husband James Harvey died in California where he had gone to recover his own health after nursing his wife and children. And so Craigdarroch became the home of a grieving widow and her orphaned grandchildren with only the unmarried status of Joan's daughters, Jessie, Annie and Maud, providing an incentive for parties and entertainments.

By the spring of 1891 she had established herself in her own second-floor suite of rooms, the only part of the castle in which she seems to have been able to feel really comfortable and at home. Her sitting room, facing south over the terraced garden, was furnished with armchairs and a settee covered in rich 'old gold' velvet.[56] Persian and Turkish carpets warmed the floor and nine

[55] *Colonist*, September 17, 1889. James Harvey's death was reported *Colonist*, February 28, 1890

[56] Descriptions of furnishings are based on the Auction Catalogue which detailed the contents. (CCA)

oil paintings, one a portrait and the others representing the four seasons and four times of day, decorated the walls.

Except for the portrait, which was probably of her husband, these and other paintings which were hung throughout the castle give the impression of having been catalogue-ordered, selected all at once as wall-coverings rather than as the result of years of careful collection. At least eight of the castle's oil paintings were the work of Frederick Schafer. A German-born artist who 'fought against alcoholism, not always successfully,'[57] Schafer seems to have been driven by a compulsion to paint every mountain on the west coast. In addition to *Morning, Mount Shasta, California*, found in Joan's sitting room, were *Donner Lake* and *Mount Tacoma* gracing the billiard room, the *California Alps* hanging in the library, *Mount of Holy Cross* and *Mount Tamalpias, California* speeding digestion in the dining room, and in the smoking room *Mount Erwin, Shasta California* and *Moonlight on the Sound* competing for attention with a set of buffalo horns.

In 1891, fifty year old Schafer had turned up in Vancouver, where he announced that he would auction off a collection of his paintings to finance the establishment of the studio and art school where he would teach 'landscape, marine and figure painting.'

'This will be appreciated by our well-to-do citizens, as ladies and gentlemen can cultivate their taste in the high arts under the instruction of this most eminent gentleman,' the *Vancouver Daily World* noted encouragingly.[58]

Schafer's auction was not a success. Many paintings, valued by the artist at two hundred dollars, were knocked down for less than the cost of their frames. And there is the tantalizing possibility that some, and perhaps most, of those paintings with their bargain-basement prices made their way to Craigdarroch.

Leaving the same impression of having been purchased in bulk were the books in Craigdarroch's library. The room itself was everything a library should be. Its stained glass windows, installed in the upper panels of the rounded bay window, served as symbolic reminders of Joan and Robert's heritage. Scotch thistles in the center panel recalled their Ayrshire birthplace. In one of the side-lights, bluebells of Scotland represented Robert's side

[57] P. and H. Samuels, *The Illustrated Biographical Encyclopedia of Artists of the American West,* 1976

[58] *Vancouver Daily World,* September 1, 1891

Lined with glass-fronted mahogany bookcases, the library is restful and dark.

of the family; in the other, English holly honoured the memory of Joan's mother, Agnes, the English-born daughter of Major Crooks, an officer in the British Army. Panelled with mahogany, and cheered by a fireplace with a flue diverted around a fourth stained glass window, the library was one of the most comfortable rooms in the house.

The order to A.H. Andrews and Company had specified glass-fronted bookcases capable of shelving over one thousand volumes. And so the library shelves were filled, not with the random and eclectic selections of a reading family, but with complete multi-volumed sets in matching Moroccan leather bindings. Not all of the library's books had been ordered to dress the shelves. Single volumes, such as *Manual for Railroad Engineers* and *Dr. Buchan's Family Physician* had no doubt been packed into boxes and carried over from 'Fairview.' *Colton vs Stanford* and *The Personal Memoirs of U.S. Grant* represented a healthy interest in the lives of men who had been Robert's business partners or acquaintances, and *Familiar Chats with Queens of the Stage* was required reading for any young girls who were as besotted with actresses and the

A large comfortable room on the castle's third floor, the billiard room must have seemed rather anacronistic in Joan Dunsmuir's all-female household.

stage as were some of Joan's granddaughters. But eight volumes of George Eliot's works, ten volumes of Thackeray, twelve volumes of Ruskin and thirty-nine volumes of Carlyle, all resplendent in 'half-Morocco binding,' would seem to have been ordered with an urge to furnish the room rather than the mind.

It wasn't as if the Dunsmuirs were philistines. Like other *nouveau-riche* Victorians, they had, of necessity, been too busy making money, too occupied with founding and consolidating a fortune, to take the time to develop cultivated taste. And they lived in an age of conspicuous acquisition; a time during which clutter and over-decoration were the hallmarks of proper interior design.

Few Victorian eyebrows would have been raised by the excesses of the castle's double drawing room. Even empty of furniture, the drawing room was so richly decorated that it seemed eye-fillingly full. Almost fifty feet long and elegantly proportioned, the room was lit during the day with the gem-like glow of seven stained glass windows and at night by two huge brass chandeliers which combined gas and electric light. Two fireplaces, each with a gilt-touched, mirrored mantel, warmed the room and hand-painted birds, garlands and bouquets covered the ceiling.

Into this room, Joan moved an interesting assortment of fur-

A well-turned-out equestrienne, Jessie Dunsmuir sits atop her equally well-groomed horse on Craigdarroch's carriage drive. Just beginning to creep up the wall is the ivy which would later threaten to envelop the castle.

niture, art work and bric-a-brac. Brocade curtains were hung at the windows and doors. The oak floors were covered with five Persian carpets and three bearskins, one cinnamon and two 'magnificent white.' Scattered about the room were an upholstered settee, five easy chairs only two of which could be described as 'very comfortable,' three 'gilded' and three upholstered occasional chairs and an 'antique, colonial, walnut settee' upholstered in silk tapestry and accompanied by three matching easy chairs. By one of the fireplaces stood a Steinway baby grand piano in a rosewood case. Japanese and Chinese vases, Watteau figures and other pieces of hand-painted china were placed about the room, but the *piece-de-resistance* was a marble statue, by 'the noted sculptor Aristide Fontana S. Carrara,' which dominated the room from its perch atop a blue marble pedestal and was, with an estimated value of $1000, the most expensive piece in the room. Craigdarroch was 'magnificent,' the *Colonist* cooed.

Craigdarroch soon proved just how successful a castle could be in luring a peripatetic aristocrat. During the years Craigdarroch was being built, Sir Richard Musgrave, an Irish baronet with

Irish baronet Sir Richard Musgrave married Jessie Dunsmuir in 1891.

an eight thousand acre Waterford estate, had begun to visit Vancouver Island to fish the Campbell River, to spend time with his younger brother Edward who operated a large sheep farm on Saltspring Island and to escape the complaints of his Irish tenants who insisted that the rents he charged were too high. Considering himself land-poor, Musgrave must have counted himself fortunate when he attracted the attention of Jessie Dunsmuir, an heiress sixteen years his junior. Although he had left a fiancee waiting in London for his return, he began a determined courtship.

On September 23, 1891 Sir Richard and Jessie were married. After the ceremony, described as 'the most fashionable and brilliant witnessed in Victoria for many months,' the castle's doors were thrown open to three hundred guests who, entertained by the band of *H.M.S. Warspite*, spent several 'merry ' hours strolling through the 'palatial residence and its beautiful grounds.'[59]

If Musgrave had married Jessie for her money and she had married him for his title, Jessie certainly got the better bargain. As Lady Musgrave she had entree to Dublin's Vice-Regal court and to the Court of St. James and the London season. Her two younger sisters took advantage of her new-found status. In Dublin in the spring of 1898, Jessie gave a ball, 'the most brilliant social event of the season,' at which she and her twenty-six year old sister Maud entertained 'the elite of the Irish capital.'[60] Two months later, on June 8, 1898 Maud was married in London to Lieutenant Reginald Spencer Chaplin of the 10th Hussars, *aide-de-camp* to Lord Roberts, Commander of Her Majesty's forces in Ireland.

Also in London two years later thirty-two year old Annie Euphemia escaped spinsterhood when on February 27, 1900 she married Commander Somerset Arthur Gough-Calthorpe, son of the 7th Baronet Calthorpe and a career naval officer who would serve as *aide-de-camp* to King George V in 1910.[61] Unlike Maud's wedding, which had been attended by a score of titled ladies including at least one Duchess, the list of invited guests who witnessed Annie Euphemia's marriage was short and relatively undistinguished. But as the society papers were quick to point out, 'Owing to a recent bereavement in the bride's family the wedding guests were confined to the immediate friends and relations of the bride and bridegroom.'

[59] *Colonist*, September 24, 1891
[60] *Colonist*, April 4, 1898
[61] *Colonist*, June 26, 1898. Annie's wedding reported *Colonist*, March 18, 1900

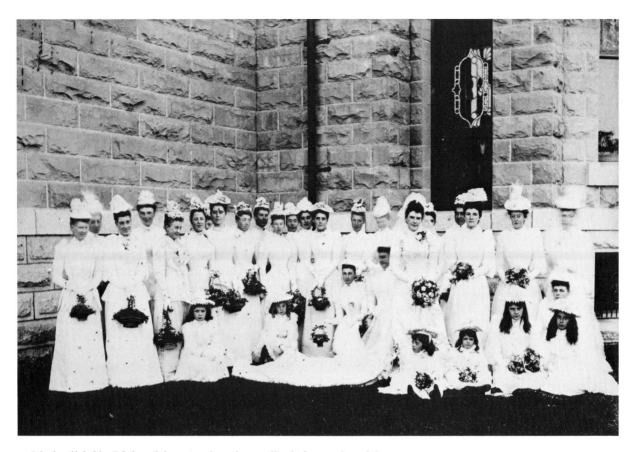

Little did Sir Richard know when he walked down the aisle of St. George's, Hanover Square to give Annie away that as a result of that recent bereavement, the Dunsmuir fortune would slip from Jessie's grasp. Neither could he have guessed that soon he and Jessie would find themselves convincing Joan to join a beautiful 'Floradora' girl in a lawsuit against Jessie's brother James which would divide the family and which would provide Victorians with an engrossing scandal as the Dunsmuirs publicly washed their dirty linen.

For this formal portrait Jessie and her entourage, thirty-one bridesmaids and flower-girls, stood in the shade of the castle's north east corner. Above them can be seen the dining room door that opens onto a four-foot drop.

The Will Case

For his sons, James and Alexander, Robert's death represented a double loss. More than a respected father, he had been the powerful boss for whom both James and Alex had worked. But if the brothers were saddened by their father's death and if they worried about assuming his role as company director, those feelings changed to frustration and perhaps to anger when Robert's will was read.

In a simple, one-page, hand-written document, the richest man in British Columbia left his entire estate — his houses and all his land, his coal mines, his coal-carriers, his steamers, his shares in Albion Iron Works, his interest in the railroad, all his goods and all his chattels — to one person — his wife Joan.[62]

More than its simplicity made Robert's will an extraordinary document. When the men with considerable estates who were his contemporaries wrote their wills, they demonstrated that they had little faith in the business acumen of their wives. Characteristically, they left their affairs in the hands of trustees, who were charged with advancing to the widow carefully directed payments from her lifetime interest in her husband's estate.[63] For Robert to have entrusted his estate to his wife was so unusual that by that act alone he demonstrated that testaments to her influence were more than empty praise. But to his sons, his will provided proof of their father's perfidy.

James and Alex had never worked for anyone other than their father. Their entire working lives had been devoted to increasing the family fortune. For this they received no set salary, neither were they given shares in any of Dunsmuir's various businesses. They were told to simply take out of the business whatever living expenses they needed. Robert was not ungenerous and both James and Alex lived well, but neither of them had anything he could really call his own and neither had an income not directly controlled by their father. They had believed his assurances that their day would come; the bulk of his estate and the control of his enterprises would be left to them; they would assume his role

[62] Last Will and Testament, Robert Dunsmuir, January 20, 1887 (photocopy, CCA)

[63] see for example, Probate Records for Trutch, Pearse, Pemberton (Probate Records, PABC)

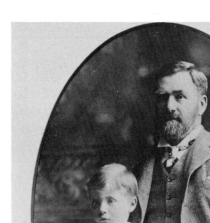

as provider to Joan and her daughters.

Even during Robert's lifetime, the arrangement had not been entirely satisfactory for it meant that their father could exercise control of their private lives. 'Take what you want,' he had said. 'Just don't want too much.'[64] So they lived well but cautiously, knowing that at any time Robert could cut off the source of their income. In addition their dependency required them to lead lives above their father's reproach for his disapproval could mean disinheritance, could result in the loss of their share of the fortune that they had devoted their lives to building.

Robert's control weighed less heavily on the older son, James. Born at Fort Vancouver on the Columbia River during his family's transit from Scotland to Vancouver Island, James was solid, careful and unimaginative. Recognizing James as the less talented of the two boys, Robert had decided that his role lay in the

Both James (left) and Alex worked hard to increase the family fortune. They believed their father's assurances that one day he would gift them with the family businesses and would leave them in full control. His last will and testament provided proof that his promises had been empty.

[64] James Dunsmuir Testimony (Attorney General's Papers, PABC)

underground management of the coal mines. James was sent to Virginia to study mining engineering. While he was there he met and married Laura Surles of North Carolina. He returned to Nanaimo with his bride in 1876 and worked in the mines until 1882 when Robert's removal to Victoria prompted a reorganization of the company. James was promoted to Departure Bay where he superintended the loading of coal at the company's docks and where he and Laura and their growing family moved into a handsome eleven room house provided by Robert.

James' dependency had not forced him to unwillingly conform to his father's wishes. He was by nature trustworthy and reliable and his parents approved of his wife Laura who proudly claimed a relationship with the aristocratic Byrd family of Virginia.

For Alex the situation was very different. Bright and quick compared to James, Alex had been his father's right hand man. In 1876 when James returned to Nanaimo after completing his studies, Alex was sent to work with Berryman and later with Diggle at the San Francisco sales office. When Diggle returned to England in 1881, Alex assumed full control.

He had been in San Francisco only a few months when he took rooms in the home of Josephine and Waller Wallace and their two children. Coyly vague about her age, but at least four years older than twenty-eight year old Alex, Josephine was a fine, full-bodied woman and Alex soon found himself in love. Waller Wallace was eased out and in 1881 Josephine obtained a divorce. She was now free to marry Alex but the very notion of his wedding a divorcee was greeted with horror by Robert and Joan. They forbade the union and informed Alex that they would refuse to receive Josephine in their home should he be so imprudent as to bring her to Victoria.

Alex and Josephine lived together, unmarried but always hoping that his parents would relent. To San Franciscans Josephine was 'Mrs Dunsmuir,' no one thinking to question the regularity of her relationship with Alex. But when Robert or any of his friends visited the city, Josephine's role as paramour was acknowledged by the necessity of Alex's hiding her away until their departure. And it may have been the pressure of leading a double life that led to the alcoholic binges in which Alex indulged with increasing frequency.

When he learned of his father's death, Alex must have felt that now, finally, after eight years of living as man and wife, he and Josephine would be free to marry. He could risk his mother's disapproval if that disapproval didn't also mean his disinheritance. But when Robert's will was read Alex realized that nothing had changed, except that now his future depended on his mother's whim rather than his father's.

And the will presented Alex with another worry, a worry that James could share. Would Joan invest the companies' profits in the acquisition of husbands for her unmarried daughters? In 1886 their sister Emily had married Northing Pinkney Snowden whose only contribution to the family's assets seems to have been his name and for whom Alex and James felt a barely concealed contempt. Only a few months after Robert's death, Emily and Snowden were making plans to move into 'Ashnola,' a large Elizabethan-style brick residence that had cost $25,000 to build and which had not been built with Snowden's money. Would they now be working to support brothers-in-law in styles to which they had no right to become accustomed?

The only solution lay in wresting some control of the businesses from Joan. It took seven years of earnest conversations, seven years of careful and cautious negotiating, before Joan agreed to give them title to the San Francisco operation. In the spring of 1896, 'R. Dunsmuir and Sons' became a joint stock company; Joan divided the shares between her two sons; and the company's name underwent a small, but significant change, becoming 'R. Dunsmuir's Sons.'[65]

Emboldened by this success, Alex and James now launched a campaign which their sister Emily would describe as 'coercion,' that resulted in their control of the Dunsmuir coal mines. On October 19, 1899, a full ten years after Robert's death, Alex and James convinced their mother than she should allow them to purchase the Wellington Collieries, the coal carriers *Wellington* and *Lorne*, all the coal in bunkers and the right to use the company name. For this they agreed to pay $410,000 over a ten year period with Joan receiving interest of five per cent on the unpaid balance.[66] That amount was too low, her daughters claimed. Alex and James had taken advantage of their mother. They had worn her down, had 'led her a miserable life' until she had finally agreed

[65] Agreement of September 3, 1896 (Attorney General's Papers, PABC)

[66] Agreement of October 16, 1899 (Attorney General's Papers, PABC)

James and Alex were not particularly thrilled that they were working hard to keep their brothers-in-law in luxury. Northing Pinkney Snowden, married to Emily, lived at 'Ashnola' which stood on the waterfront surrounded by extensive grounds and which had not been build with Snowden's money.

to sell. James and Alex countered by pointing out that Joan had taken more than three million dollars out of the business since 1889 and since much of that money had been disbursed to the girls in the form of trusts, they felt that their sisters had no real cause for complaint.

Two months after Joan put her signature to the agreement, Alex married Josephine. Josephine, who had spent almost twenty years waiting for Alex to marry her, would be his legal wife for less than six weeks. On January 31, 1900 while honeymooning in New York, Alex died. He was forty-six years old. Required to assign a cause of death, his doctors hedged. 'Meningitis' was entered on his death certificate, but, as it soon became apparent, Alex had been a confirmed alcoholic and had died of acute alcoholic poisoning.

When the contents of Alex's will were revealed, the simmering family feud erupted into open warfare. When Joan had given them the San Francisco business she had extracted from both Alex and James a promise that if either of them died, his share would revert to her. But in a will signed within an hour of his marriage to Josephine, Alex had left everything to his brother James.

Alex had been incompetent, his sisters charged. He was a drunkard who hadn't known what he was doing and who had been controlled and manipulated by James. Pressured by her daughters, Joan decided to challenge Alex's will by claiming that in leaving the San Francisco operation to James, Alex had acted in contravention of the agreement she had with her sons.

Members of the richest family in the province arguing publicly over the division of the fortune would have been spectacle enough to enthrall Victorians. But James had followed his father into politics and on June 16, 1900 had been elected Premier of British Columbia. His embarrassment at being sued by Joan must have been acute and his elevated position only increased public enjoyment of the case.

'Premier of British Columbia Sued by his Mother,' the *New York Times* trumpeted.[67]

Joan and her daughters soon discovered that they were not alone in their dissatisfaction with the terms of the will. Alex had entrusted Josephine's welfare to his brother. Josephine would retain title to the mansion in San Leandro, near Oakland, which Alex had built for her shortly before his death. But Josephine would be dependent on James for any income she received from Alex's estate. In return for a monthly payment of $2000, Josephine agreed not to contest her husband's will. The agreement was kept secret from her daughter Edna who presumed her mother to be a wealthy woman.

Edna Wallace had lived with her mother and Alex until 1891 when she had gone to New York to pursue a theatrical career. A beautiful girl with a gift for comedy, she had been an instant success, landing a leading role in 'Panjandrum' and landing the leading man, DeWolf Hopper, the most popular stage comedian of the day. When, eighteen months after burying Alex, Josephine succumbed to breast cancer, Edna flitted back to San Leandro, thinking herself an heiress. 'Edna Wallace inherits a fortune of which her share runs into six figures,' the *San Francisco Examiner* breathlessly reported.[68]

When Edna discovered that Josephine's cooperation had been bought so cheaply, she hurried back to New York, hired the best lawyer she could find and took James Dunsmuir to court. Joan was now faced with a dilemma. She had been contesting only

Insisting that James had exercised undue influence over his alcoholic brother, Joan took her son to court.

[67] *New York Times*, November 10, 1901
[68] *San Francisco Examiner*, June 24, 1901

Alexander Dunsmuir's step-daughter Edna Wallace Hopper was a popular musical-comedienne and the toast of the turn-of-the-century New York stage. Edna thought that she would inherit Alexander's estate. When she discovered that that was not the case, she took his brother James to court. The case dragged on for over four years. In the end Edna received only the mansion Alexander had built for her mother in 1899 at San Leandro near Oakland.

Alex's right to dispose of the San Francisco property; Edna was intent on having the entire will set aside. Could she protect her own interests without becoming involved in the case? Or would she be forced to cooperate with the child of 'that woman'?

Finally, pressured by her daughters and in particular by Jessie, Joan entered the action and for years newspapers in Victoria, San Francisco and New York treated their readers to detailed accounts of the most extraordinary testimony, much of it dealing with Alex's enormous capacity for alcohol. The case dragged on until 1906 when the last appeals were exhausted. The will was upheld; James would retain his brother's share of the fortune; Joan and her daughters would receive nothing and Edna had to be content with the income she received from the sale of the San Leandro estate.

White Elephant

By the time the will case was settled James Dunsmuir had given up his political career and had accepted appointment as Lieutenant Governor. As the King's representative in British Columbia, James was in residence at Government House when he learned that the will case had been decided in his favour. His fortune secure he began to make plans for a future which now seemed exceedingly bright and which included the construction of a castle of his own.

For a few years after his mother had moved into Craigdarroch, James and his family had taken up residence in 'Fairview.' In 1892 he had moved into 'Burleith' the large, rambling Queen Anne mansion that had been built for him on twenty waterfront acres. At first he had thought that after leaving Government House he would return to 'Burleith' and in 1907 he had ordered an architect to begin preparing plans for its renovation. But with the settlement of the will case, James had the money he needed to fulfill his ambition to live like a member of the landed gentry and when he learned that two hundred and fifty acres of country land was being offered for sale he acted quickly. By 1908, when he began the construction of his estate, he had acquired more than six hundred acres of field and forest fronting on the Esquimalt Lagoon.

Planned by Victoria's pre-eminent residential architect, Samuel Maclure, the mansion at 'Hatley Park' was on 'a scale of magnificence never equalled in the West.' Designed as a medieval castle with tudor additions, 'Hatley' was meant to appear as if it had been standing for centuries.

For James Dunsmuir the years he spent planning 'Hatley' should have been exceptionally happy ones. Obliged to become involved in the coal business by family expectations, he was now about to fulfill his dream of becoming a gentleman farmer, and as he began to divest himself of his businesses so that he could spend his days hunting and fishing and managing his estate, there can be little doubt that he was enjoying a degree of unusual contentment. But tugging at his peace of mind was his continuing

After he completed his term as Lieutenant Governor, James Dunsmuir thought that he would return to 'Burleith,' his sprawling Queen Anne house on the waterfront in Victoria West. But after the settlement of the will case, he decided to buy several hundred acres of land on the Esquimalt Lagoon and build 'Hatley,' a dream-castle of his own.

Designed as a medieval castle with tudor additions 'Hatley' was meant to appear as if it had been standing for centuries. In 1940 the house and the seven hundred acres of land that went with it were sold to the Department of National Defence. Now part of the campus of Royal Roads Military College, 'Hatley' is usually open to the public during the summer months.

alienation from his mother.

James had tried to heal the wounds that the extended legal case had caused by offering to pay all the court costs incurred by his mother and sisters. And he had called at Craigdarroch, hat in hand, hoping that his mother would agree to see him.

'I was told that if I went up to see my mother the door would be shut in my face,' James recalled.

Over eighty years old and in failing health, Joan must have recognized that her time was short. But she remained adamant. She would not see James. She went to her grave unreconciled with her only surviving son.

So deep had the family division become, that at first James decided not to attend her funeral but at the last minute he changed his mind and mourners shifted uncomfortably in their seats when the Lieutenant Governor, sobbing loudly, 'broke down' during the service.[69]

In headlining Joan's death, the *Daily Colonist* described her as a pioneer, and that characterization she certainly merited. There were few women still living who could claim that their first years on Vancouver Island had been spent in a little clamshell-floored cabin, without window glass and with constant draughts fingering their way through the chinks in the squared-log walls. Joan Dunsmuir represented more than just a link with the frontier past; in her rise from cabin to castle, she symbolized the great changes that had taken place in the province. Many of the mourners at her funeral were aware that they were witnessing the passing of an era.

They were also witnessing the passing of a singular woman. 'She possessed a mind of more than ordinary vigor and a keen sense of duty, combined with great fearlessness,' the *Colonist* editorialized. 'She was a welcome visitor in every home where there was a need for a clear brain, willing hands and a heart full of sympathy.'[70]

Some of the 'humbler mourners' were anxious to recall Joan's 'unremitting kindnesses.' An 'old lady in reduced circumstances' said that for more than twenty years 'she had had to thank Mrs. Dunsmuir every week for help and kindnesses.' One old miner had walked twenty-eight miles to Victoria to attend her funeral and his story encouraged the *Colonist* to become positively

[69] *Vancouver Province*, October 6, 1908
[70] *Colonist*, October 3, 1908

Joan Dunsmuir's death was front page news in the *Colonist*. The rival paper, the *Victoria Times* did not consider the news nearly so momentous. (*Colonist*, October 3, 1908)

maudlin. 'It was a story of unselfish kindness taking thought to alleviate the burdens which sickness brings upon the poor, and of the last hours of a loved one lightened with those attentions which only money can buy, the inability to provide which is the cruelest blow which unkind fortune can deal.'[71]

If, during her lifetime, Joan had not been known as a benefactress that was simply because her charity had been dispensed with an 'unostentatious hand,' the *Colonist* assured its readers. It was

[71] *Colonist,* October 6, 1908

odd, then, that in her will Joan left nothing to charity and made no special bequests to those who had depended on her and who had been so willing to testify to her benevolence.

Except for small bequests to two friends and to her servants, Joan left everything to her five surviving daughters.[72] James was, of course, excluded from the will, but he may have noted with pleasure that so too were his brothers-in-law. Joan's estate was to be held in trust and divided into five equal shares. Each daughter would receive a lifetime interest from her share. That share would be transferred to her children upon her death and if she died childless would revert to her sisters.

None of Joan's daughters, each of whom had received a one-fifth share of the castle, its contents and its grounds,[73] was prepared to buy the others out and take title to Craigdarroch, and so Joan's trustees decided that the house and everything that went with it would be sold as soon as her will cleared probate.

During a three day sale, beginning on June 21, 1909, the castle's furnishings — everything from toast racks to tea sets, from curtain rods to carpets, everything from silver plated stair rods to stepladders, from the Steinway baby grand to wheelbarrows and garden tools — were sold at public auction. Joan's 'Magnificent Antique Colonial Black Walnut Bedroom Suite' sold for $110.00; the "Elaborate, well-made, full-sized English Billiard Table, in first-class condition, manufactured by Burrows & Watts of London' brought $425.00; a 'gilded occasional chair' sold for $11.00; and an 'Antique Colonial Walnut Stool, upholstered in silk' went for $5.50.[74]

Finding new homes for the furniture proved easier than finding new occupants for the house. On June 5, 1909 the *Colonist* carried the front page news that the castle and its grounds had been sold. The happy purchaser was chartered accountant, Griffith R. Hughes who cheerfully announced plans for a subdivision of 144 lots in addition to the two acre plot which would stay with the castle. 'The consideration was well up in the hundreds of thousands,' the *Colonist* inaccurately reported.

Hughes had reached an unusual arrangement with Joan's daughters. Rather than purchasing the estate, it seems that he had agreed to act as agent in the sale of the lots or it may be that the five girls had agreed to sell, but had required from Hughes

Attending his mother's funeral in his official capacity as Lieutenant Governor, James Dunsmuir broke down during the service, overcome by the thought that during the last years of her life Joan had refused to speak to him.

[72] Last Will and Testament, Joan Dunsmuir, November 8, 1906 (Probate Records, PABC)

[73] An Indenture dated March 14, 1908 and registered June 9, 1910 in Absolute Fees Book shows that Joan sold Craigdarroch and other parcels of land in the City of Victoria to her five daughters for two dollars. If this was an attempt to avoid succession duties it seems to have failed for at least some of these properties were included in the valuation of Joan's estate.

[74] Auction Catalogue, (photocopy, CCA)

Famous Victoria Landmark Changed Hands Yesterday

"Craigdarroch" Sold to Mr. Griffith R. Hughes—His Intention is to Sub-Divide the Property

On June 5, 1909 the *Colonist* carried the news that Craigdarroch had found a buyer who intended to turn the grounds into the city's most exclusive subdivision.

[75] Indenture, April 1, 1910 (Land Registry, Victoria)

no payment until he had sold enough of the property to finance the purchase of the rest. Whatever the case, Hughes was certainly not the legal owner, when in June 9, 1909 the lots were first offered for sale.

The full page advertisements which appeared in local newspapers appealed to potential purchasers with promises of view lots, guaranteed cleared and free of stone.

'What the DERBY is to the racing world! What the MARATHON is to the athlete! Such is "CRAIGDARROCH" to the man who desires an absolutely perfect site for his residence or the sound investment of his money!!'

That was one of the more modest statements made in an attempt to lure Victorians to Craigdarroch, but in spite of the appeal of the sites and in spite of the aggressive advertising campaign, sales were slow, so slow that a new approach had to be developed.

Hughes decided to appeal to purchasers' gambling instincts. Prices were set at a flat $2750 per lot. Specific lots could not be purchased; instead lots would be assigned to individual buyers by chance. For $2750 a purchaser's name was entered in a lottery and while he knew he would own part of the Craigdarroch subdivision, he would not know which part until the evening of March 26, 1910 when the draw would be held. As an added incentive, Hughes announced that a second draw would be held and one of the lucky lot-owners would win the castle, which, he admitted had been 'difficult to dispose of.'

The lottery and its prize proved successful in attracting ninety-nine purchasers who bought a total of 120 lots.[75] Some of the purchasers intended to build. John Welbore Spencer bought three lots near his father's home, 'Lan Dderwan,' which stood on several acres of land between Rockland and Fort Street. Others obviously regarded the lots as speculative investments and many of the town's realtors were prepared to take a chance on acquiring one of the subdivision's more spectacular lots and on winning Dunsmuir Castle. By far the most interesting purchaser was James Dunsmuir's wife Laura who may have found the possibility of winning her mother-in-law's castle well-nigh irresistible.

'The drawing took place at the castle, the greatest interest being naturally shown by all interested parties, and by many out-

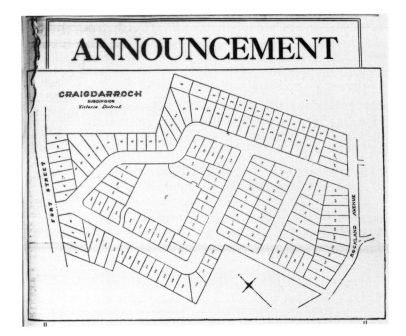

With one larger parcel set aside for the castle's grounds, the twenty-eight acre Dunsmuir estate was carved into 144 separate lots. (*Colonist*, June 9, 1909)

siders who flocked to Craigdarroch,' the Colonist reported.[76] The lucky winner was Solomon Cameron who might have seen it as something of an omen that he had also drawn Lot 13.

With the lots assigned and the castle won, Hughes busied himself legalizing the transactions. In an unusual document dated April 1, 1910,[77] Jessie, Mary Jean, Emily Ellen, Annie Euphemia and Henrietta Maud agreed to sell the property to Hughes. In addition to an initial payment of $30,000 they would receive $1,750 for each lot that had already been spoken for. Without apparently having had to make any significant investment, Hughes would receive a profit of one thousand dollars for each lot. Even after he had deducted the up-front payment of $30,000, he was still left with $90,000 to cover expenses he had incurred in arranging the sales. The Dunsmuir sisters stood to receive $240,000 but once that was divided into five shares and then locked into individual trusts, not one of them would do so well as Hughes.

Solomon Cameron received title to the castle on November 10, 1910 and wasted no time in marching down to his bank to find

[76] B.W. Davies, 'Craigdarroch Castle' (typescript, CCA)

[77] Indenture (Land Registry, Victoria)

During the latter part of June, 1909, full-page advertisements in Victoria newspapers lured purchasers to Craigdarroch.

out just how how much money a castle was capable of raising. The owner of the Westholme Lumber Company, Cameron had decided to dabble in some serious property speculation. He had already bought, or was in the process of buying, up to half a dozen lots in the townsite of Prince Rupert, a stump-city which was expected to boom once the Grand Trunk Pacific Railroad completed construction of its trans-continental rail line and Prince Rupert became its west coast terminus. By November 19th Craigdarroch had its first mortgage and Cameron had $25,000 to invest in a few thousand square feet of rocks and mud.[78]

Craigdarroch could be a chilly residence for anyone who didn't have an unlimited supply of coal, and it seems that Solomon Cameron decided against moving into the castle himself. Instead he installed a relative to act as caretaker and Craigdarroch became a 'white elephant,' neglected and slipping gradually into a state of dereliction and decay.

'Crippled Heroes'

Even before Craigdarroch had been won by Solomon Cameron, it had begun to assume a rather seedy appearance. Margaret Holmes was fifteen when her family moved to a house on Yates Street in 1909. 'The mansion was very much deserted,' she recalled. 'Nobody seemed to be looking after it.'[79]

'The garden was neglected. You could see it had been rather beautiful and people had been using it as a place to go walking in, and picking wildflowers. It was very beautiful because you got such a lovely view of the city. You'd see the spires of the cathedral and the Sooke hills . . . and Trial Island. It was an unobstructed view, perfectly beautiful.'

Craigdarroch's derelict gardens would become inextricably linked in her memory with the arrival of Halley's comet in 1910. 'Quite a crowd of people went and sat out on the edge of the terrace. You got a clear view of the western sky where you were supposed to see the comet.'

The castle's condition certainly didn't improve during the years of the Cameron family's tenancy. And the grounds, although subdivided and sold, remained an almost wild, natural park. The years before the First World War were marked by manic land speculation. Properties sold and re-sold at ever increasing prices. Below the Rockland heights, Chinese market gardens were plowed up, orchards were cut down and in their places dozens of stout Edwardian bungalows appeared, marching along newly-opened streets from Rockland to the sea. But in that pool of frantic ac-

(*Colonist*, June 19, 1948)

[78] Certificate of Indefeasible Title, August, 1910 (Land Registry, Victoria)

[79] Miss Margaret Holmes, Interview, October 25, 1985 (tape, CCA)

Dunsmuir Castle. VICTORIA B.C.

Its flower beds untended and knee-high grass waving on its once-manicured terraces, Craigdarroch began to assume an air of genteel decay during Solomon Cameron's tenancy.

tivity, Craigdarroch's acres remained an island of calm. By 1913 only three houses had been built in the subdivision and only nine more were built in 1914, the year that marked the beginning of the war and the end of the building boom.

The beginning of the war also meant the end to Prince Rupert's bright future. The railway reached the city in 1914 but the projected boom did not materialize, as energies that might have been put into building the town and increasing the rail line's profits were redirected to the war effort. Solomon Cameron found his Prince Rupert lots almost valueless. Deeply in debt, Cameron hung on, hoping that peace would bring with it a return to prosperity. But prosperity, when it came, came too late for Cameron. On May 26, 1919 the Bank of Montreal began to take legal steps toward foreclosure and with the pending action registered against the title and having no hope of raising the capital to redeem the mortgage, Cameron and the castle officially parted company.[80]

Their separation had been evident several months earlier, when on January 30, 1919 G. H. Deane, assistant director of the Soldiers' Civil Re-establishment Board announced that the castle would be taken over by the federal government and would be operated as a vocational training center for men returning from overseas.[81] The kitchen would be upgraded, the plumbing 'extended' and the castle would be ready for occupancy within six weeks, Deane predicted.

The act establishing the Department of Soldiers' Civil Re-establishment had been passed by the federal government on May 24, 1918 as the number of soldiers returning to Canada, either desperately ill or severely disabled, had climbed into the thousands. Specialized hospitals would be needed for their care. And some kind of training would be required for other soldiers who were not totally incapacitated but whose injuries prevented them from returning to their pre-war occupations.

The department ran vocational training centers, most of which functioned as day centers with soldiers attending on an out-patient basis, but no evidence suggests that this type of facility was ever planned for Craigdarroch. Instead the castle would become a hospital and would fall into one of the three categories established by the department for the treatment of soldiers who had, in turn, been categorized 'according to the nature of disease or ailment' such as 'wounds, general diseases, tuberculosis, insanity, feeble-mindedness, epileptics, neurological, orthopaedic, dental, venereal.'[82] Craigdarroch might have become a tubercular hospital or it might have become an asylum for the insane; but instead it became one of three hospitals in Canada providing care for 'long-treatment cases and incurables.'

The departmental report provided a chilling description of the patients the castle was being readied to receive. 'The patients in these institutions are mostly men who, for example, have been shot through the spinal column and are partly or completely paralyzed.' But, the report continued brightly, 'It is interesting

[80] The Bank of Montreal received title to the castle September 14, 1921, Certificate of Indefeasible Title (Land Registry, Victoria)

[81] *Colonist*, January 30, 1919

[82] Annual Report, Department of Soldiers' Civil Re-establishment, *Sessional Papers*, 1920

Edward, Prince of Wales, pictured here with the Lieutenant Governor's wife Lady Barnard, visited Victoria in September of 1919 as part of his around-the-Empire good will tour. On the first day of his visit he unveiled his grandmother's statue on the lawns of the legislative buildings. On the second, he opened the military hospital at Craigdarroch.

to note that a not inconsiderable proportion of those ordinarily described as "incurable" respond satisfactorily to occupational treatment . . .'

That presumably was the rationale behind the construction of an annex designed by Victoria architect William D'Oyly Rochfort. A one-storey building, embellished with tudor decorative elements, the annex stood on the terraced lawn below the castle. 'A very picturesque little addition to the grounds,' it was designed to house a machine shop, a wood-working room and a 'basket room.'

"Perseverance in treatment towards cure in these hospitals for long treatment is considered preferable to placing patients ordinarily classed as "incurable" in homes for incurables to await tediously the end of their lives,' the departmental report noted.

During the summer of 1919, while the annex was being built, the castle was being torn apart. 'The whole interior has undergone thorough renovation and cleaning in preparation for its new use,' the department proudly announced.[83] The library would continue to be used as a library, the dining room would remain a dining room and the double drawing room would be used as a recreation room. But those seem to have been the only rooms to have

[83] *Sessional Papers*, 1920

escaped unscathed. 'Whole walls have had to be torn down to extend some of the rooms,' the *Colonist* reported.[84] A new steam heating plant had been installed; a hydro-therapy room had been located in the basement; and a fire-escape now clung to the outside walls.

The hospital was completed and patients had been moved into place just in time to allow the future King to officially open the building. Edward, Prince of Wales, was visiting Victoria as part of his around-the-Empire good will tour. On the evening of September 24, 1919 the Prince was entertained at a ball at the Empress Hotel attended by thirteen hundred prominent Victorians. Of passing interest was the fact that the Prince's presence had brought both sides of the unreconciled Dunsmuir family into the same room. One of Joan's daughters and several of her Bryden and Harvey grandchildren were in attendance as were six of James Dunsmuir's daughters who as well as outnumbering the rival camp also appeared at the top of the guest list.

The following morning the 'Sailor Prince' arrived at the castle and acknowledged the cheers of hundreds of Victorians in 'his pleasant unassuming manner.' Leaving his official car outside the grounds, he walked up the driveway and under an arch decorated with laurel leaves, fir branches, and purple and white bunting.

'Radiantly happy, fresh and neatly attired in his naval uniform,' Edward entered through the castle's west door to begin his inspection of the building. He climbed to the top of the tower to take full advantage of the view and he was conducted into a few of the wards which housed the less disabled patients.

'All the up-patients were standing to their beds. Four warriors who were badly injured remained in bed,' the *Times* reported.[85] The Prince 'spent considerable time in conversation with the crippled heroes who are now making the castle their home.'

And then he was gone and the hospital's doors were thrown open to the hundreds of people who had gathered to catch a glimpse of the Prince and now took the opportunity to have a good look at the hospital. Not surprisingly the one feature that the visitors found most impressive was the hospital's kitchen. The Department of Soldiers' Re-establishment placed a high priority on food. Each hospital was to have its own resident dietician

In the only known photograph of the Prince at Craigdarroch, Edward, wearing a white naval officer's cap, can be glimpsed as he enters the castle under the red ensign.

[84] *Colonist*, September 13, 1919
[85] *Victoria Times*, September 25, 1919

because, as a departmental report argued, 'A competent dietician is worth her entire salary for aesthetic reasons alone.'

'Who can estimate in money what it means to have: —
(a) Hot foods served hot and on hot plates;
(b) Cold foods served cold on chilled plates;
(c) Gravies, soups, sauces, and in fact all foods properly seasoned and flavoured;
(d) Foods served in moderate quantities, attractively spaced on the plate instead of being "splashed on."

Who indeed? But to get hot meals on hot plates to one hundred and ten patients arranged in wards from the castle's second to fourth floors had required the installation of a 'massive range' in the kitchen and the development of a highly organized delivery system which resulted in an unusual adaptation of some of the castle's bedrooms. A dumb-waiter ran from the basement, through the pantry and up to the floors above. And on each floor a 'serving room' was fitted with appliances for keeping the food warm after it had been sent up.

After marvelling at the modern efficiency of the dumb-waiter and noting that the vegetable gardens on the terrace were producing a crop capable of feeding the hospital's residents for some time to come, the visitors left, confident that the seven full time nurses were more than able to give the men the constant care they were said to require. As a departmental report cheerily noted, 'In a recent inspection the men, in spite of their unfortunate condition, seemed happy and contented.'[86]

Not all the men confined to Craigdarroch fell into the incurable category. Some were amputees who, after their stumps had healed and were judged to have 'properly shrunk,' were fitted with artificial legs and were spending their hospital days learning how to walk and once they could walk, learning how to dance.

Victoria girls, who were encouraged to volunteer as dancing partners, regarded the socials held in the castle's drawing room as a patriotic duty rather than a pleasure. 'They used to hold dances,' one young lady remembered. 'Well, it was good therapy for them. But have you ever tried dancing with a one-legged man?'[87]

[86] Sessional Papers, 1920
[87] Holmes, Interview

Some of the men seemed not to properly appreciate the contribution of the volunteer ladies, one of whom recalled, 'Some of them were a bit contemptuous and some of them were a bit . . well . . er . . well you didn't want to make friends with them but you didn't mind dancing with them. It was good for them.'

Craigdarroch's life as a hospital lasted only two years. In 1921 it was decided to concentrate the remaining patients into fewer, larger institutions. The 'Craig Darroch Hospital' in Victoria was one of seven institutions across Canada closed as a result of the new policy. By 1921, the Bank of Montreal, which had been receiving something in the neighbourhood of $20,000 a year in rents from the hospital, received notice of the government's in-

With its back porch glassed-in to serve as a sun porch, the castle was operating as 'Craig Darroch Military Hospital' when this photograph was taken in 1920.

tention to vacate. At about the same time they finally received legal title to the building.[88] But if the management of the bank thought that they had gained ownership of a problem building, and worse, of an empty problem building, they must have been pleasantly surprised to discover that another tenant was waiting expectantly in the wings.

Victoria College

Founded in 1903 as an affiliate of McGill University in Montreal, Victoria College suffered a setback in 1915 when, after the opening of the new University of British Columbia in Vancouver, it was decided that it was no longer necessary to offer first and second year course work in Victoria. For five years Dr. Edward Burness Paul, principal of Victoria High School and the college's founder, campaigned to have the college reinstated. In 1920 he succeeded in having the decision reversed and Victoria College once again opened its doors to students. But those doors were to the third floor classrooms of the new high school building on Grant Street — an arrangement 'not to the best advantage of either High School or College.'[89] Dr. Paul couldn't help but gaze longingly, and perhaps covetously, at the castle on the hill. When he learned that the veterans' hospital would be closed, he seized the opportunity.

Beds, dressers and wheelchairs were trundled down Craigdarroch's steps and chairs, desks, benches, tables, book shelves and blackboards were carried in. The double drawing room, with a blackboard blocking its fine gold and white fireplace, became two classrooms, the purview of the history and English teachers. Across the hall, the library was converted into the registrar's office. The dining room, crowded with the slatted benches which were notorious for their lack of comfort, became the mathematics classroom. French classes were conducted, appropriately enough, in a second floor bedroom. And the ballroom, on Craigdarroch's fourth floor and a breathtaking seventy-one steps above the first floor, became the college library.

Throughout the castle, hints to its most recent former role re-

When this photograph, found in the Victoria College 1923-1924 Annual was taken, Craigdarroch had been serving as a college campus for over a year.

[88] see note 80

[89] Public Schools Report, 1920-21 (VF-PABC)

This photograph, taken before the decorated ceiling was painted over during the 1930's, shows the drawing room converted into a classroom with a blackboard blocking the mirrored fireplace.

mained. WARD 2 was clearly stencilled in black on the door to the room designed as Joan Dunsmuir's second floor sitting room, which now housed the Men's Common Room. Other rooms were identified as the DISPENSARY and the DIETARY KITCHEN. And in the basement was a mysterious off-limits chamber which bore the designation HYDROTHERAPY ROOM. But other than those reminders, any lingering hospital gloom was soon dispelled by youthful energy and high spirits.

Many of the college's freshmen, bright students who had been permitted to skip grades and who had graduated from high school a year or two before their contemporaries, were almost ridiculously young.

'I was just sixteen when I registered at Victoria College,' one co-ed recalled. 'My two years were very exciting; they were a series of firsts — first date, first long dress, first dances with boys . . .'[90]

[90] Unless otherwise indicated recollections are drawn from Responses to Questionnaire, Victoria College Craigdarroch Students (CCA)

Crowded with benches, the dining room became the mathematics classroom.

'There were "opening of school" dances, parents tea dances, Halloween dances, Barn dances, Christmas dances, Co-ed dances when the girls treated the fellows . . ,' another student remembered, as she looked fondly back over fifty years. And no wonder the memories are so warm and vivid for there can be few colleges capable of providing so romantic a setting for undergraduate merriment.

Dances were held in the drawing room with the orchestra set up beside the piano, which stood by the window near the fireplace. As the girls arrived, they skittered up the stairs to the women's locker room on the second floor. Hair combed and dresses arranged, they then made their 'entrance' gliding gracefully down the grand staircase under the appraising eyes of their escorts and the stag line, and quite aware of the effect they were making. Asked to describe his happiest memory of the college more than forty years later, one man unhesitatingly replied, 'A beautiful girl coming down the staircase in a red dress.'

As well as a romantic setting, the castle provided an ideal setting for romance. In theory upstairs classrooms were off-limits

The dining room-cum-mathematics classroom was pressed into use as a lounge for college dances.

on dance nights; in practice they became cosy havens for 'the sweet innocent ardour of youth,' perhaps made even sweeter by the danger presented by patrolling professors.

'My date and I went upstairs to "pitch a little woo",' a co-ed reminisced. 'Every classroom we looked into was crammed with necking couples. I wouldn't go amongst so crowded a place, so we were ambling down a short hallway on the third floor when Gerald Fields appeared upstairs on the lookout for such goings on and spied us. My date seized my hand and led me hurtling down the back stairs while Mr Fields raced down the main staircase. When we hit the first floor, we walked sedately into the ballroom and were dancing by the door as Mr Fields rushed up. We smiled politely. He said nothing. He was a good sort.'

Gerald Fields was not the only teacher who students recognized as being a good sort. In 1921 when the college moved to Craigdarroch, the entire staff was composed of only six teachers responsible for imparting knowledge to a student body which numbered just over 160 students. Small classes and the cosy, clut-

Dr. Edward B. Paul served as the first principal of Victoria College during its time at Craigdarroch. A chubby man with bright blue eyes and drooping yellowed moustaches, he continued as principal of the college until he was seventy-seven.

⁹¹ Freddy Wood, cited by Peter L. Smith, *Come Give A Cheer! One Hundred Years of Victoria High School 1876-1976* (Victoria: Victoria High School Centennial Celebrations Committee, 1976)

tered informality of the castle, allowed students and faculty to observe each other closely and to get to know each other well. Craigdarroch's teachers emerged as unique, somewhat eccentric, individuals who are fondly remembered for the missionary zeal, the inspired and inspiring enthusiasm, which they brought to the teaching of their subjects.

The first principal was Dr. E. B. Paul, the endearingly chubby old gentleman with drooping white moustaches, who had championed the college's move to the castle. Dr. Paul taught Latin and Greek and something more. 'As a gracious person, he unconsciously aroused in his students an awareness of good form in the art of living.'⁹¹

Dignified and recognized as having 'a wonderful mind,' Dr. Paul won even more admiration from his students when he tangled with Judge Gregory. The judge, who lived near the castle, was inordinately proud of the carefully tended boulevard in front of his home and should any college student take a short cut across that lawn, Gregory was ready to pounce on the culprit with loud complaints. On one occasion the culprit was Dr. Paul.

'Are you speaking to me in your official capacity or just as man-to-man,' Dr. Paul demanded.

'Oh, of course, just as man-to-man, Dr. Paul,' Gregory replied, perhaps rather nonplussed to discover the identity of the trespasser.

'Well, as man-to-man, you can go to hell,' Dr. Paul thundered and walked on.

Dr. Paul retired from his duties as principal in 1927 when he was seventy-seven. He stayed on to teach a dwindling number of classical scholars. To some he was 'an ancient man teaching an ancient language,' but others saw him as 'a dear old soul' who retained his droll sense of humour when a lesser man might have become discouraged as he witnessed the declining interest in the subjects which had been his life's work. By 1929 his class of second year Greek managed to attract only three students, one of whom recalls the day that Dr. Paul entered the room and, after noting that only two students were present, gruffly declared, 'I see that fully a third of the class is absent today.' And then let out a big chuckle.

The man who replaced Dr. Paul as principal was a very dif-

ferent sort. Dr. Percy Elliott had been a boxing champion during his student years at McGill. With 'a noticeably long stride and a springing step,' Elliott was recognized as 'a real man who could tell some great stories — and often did.' Students in Elliott's chemistry and physics classes delighted in the ease with which he could be diverted from 'scientific science.' The principles behind onshore and offshore breezes might be illustrated by the distinct aroma that travelled from the well-known but illegal still that operated on the waterfront near Bamberton. And he was quite prepared to become involved in serious discussions regarding the chemical and physical considerations for putting cream in a tea-cup before or after pouring the tea.

All the teachers wore academic gowns, at least for the first few weeks of each term, but none wore them to such advantage as did Madame Sanderson-Mongin. Stout and with her wiry grey hair brushed impatiently back off her face, Sorbonne-trained Madame Sanderson-Mongin knew a thing or two about Gallic flair. On her an academic gown became a theatrical costume, flowing cloak-like behind her as she swept into a room, wrapping itself closely around her body as she shrank from a particularly bad translation and sagging from her shoulders as she crumpled half way to the floor in one of the mock fainting fits for which she

Forced to sit still for a formal photograph, Madame Sanderson-Mongin could appear rather stern and severe. But in action she effervesced, her enthusiasm for teaching and for her students bubbling over with dramatic Gallic flair.

was renowned.

'Energetic and effervescent,' Madame took an avid interest in the college's social life. With her pince-nez firmly clamped on her nose, she organized the committees that planned the college dances. And when all the balloons had been inflated and all the streamers hung, when all the benches had been removed from the castle's drawing room and piled in the hall or on the porch and when the orchestra had gathered around the piano, Madame Sanderson-Mongin, in a cloud of bonhomie with a long scarf floating behind her, would sweep into the makeshift ballroom and begin the festivities by fixing an embarrassed member of the stag line with a coquettish gaze and demanding, 'Dancez-vous, Monsieur?' in a tone that suggested that she would not take 'No' for an answer.

Walter Gage joined the faculty in 1927. At twenty-two, only a few years older than his students, and appearing almost impossibly young, Gage quickly became the college's best-loved teacher. Given the dual role of teaching mathematics and acting as the college's registrar, Gage approached his duties with the engaging panache that would continue to mark his long academic career. The 'merry nonsense' he brought to his mathematics courses convinced students that he had jokes written in the margins of his texts. 'You never slept in his classes,' one student recalled. Neither did you talk nor lark about, for Gage had the uncanny ability to spin away from the blackboard and with a single motion hurl the chalk he was holding directly at the cause of any disturbance. 'He never misses,' students reported with awe.

As registrar, Gage gave students' interests a most unbureaucratically high priority. One young man, who would go on to McGill medical school, credited Gage with speeding him on his academic way. He had failed English and he had also failed to write the supplemental exam, a state of affairs that he blamed at least in part on his dislike for the English teacher, the severe, unbending Miss Cann.

At the closing dance of the school year, Gage strolled over to him. 'You didn't write your English supp.,' he said conversationally. No, the student replied. He was going to study all summer and write it in the fall. 'I don't believe it,' Gage laughed. 'If you see 50% on your report, will you keep quiet about it?'

W.H. GAGE, REGISTRAR
MATHEMATICS

Only twenty-two when he first appeared in the Victoria College Annual, mathematics teacher Walter Gage went on to have a distinguished academic career which included a term as the much-loved president of the University of British Columbia.

And one premedical student, who knew how to keep his mouth shut, soon discovered that the record clearly showed that he had conquered second year English.

As the college's castle years passed, some students, who had clambered up its stairs and who had scratched their names into its woodwork, returned to Craigdarroch as teachers. Sydney Pettit had attended the college in 1927 and had served as editor of the annual in which he was described as 'a cynic [who] worships at the shrine of G.B.S. and utters profound statements at the slightest provocation — a really deep thinker.' His worst vice, during his student years, was 'strong tobacco, consumed in enormous quantities.' Ten years later, when he joined the staff as history teacher and librarian, some library-users found his positive mania for knowing the correct time a far more memorable characteristic than the aroma of stale tobacco which followed him about the room.

Pettit didn't wear a watch and there was no clock in the library, so he drifted around the tables, absent-mindedly cleaning his glasses on his tie and interrupting studying students to ask them the time. Finally a plot was hatched and Pettit found a large and elaborately wrapped pocket watch sitting on his desk. Quickly grasping the significance of this unexpected gift, the librarian finessed the plotters by becoming even more obsessed with the correct time which he insisted on determining with absolute precision. He continued to wander about the library but now he ostentatiously wound his new watch and every few minutes he paused to bend over book-absorbed students to murmur a variation on 'I make it 2:46. What do you have?'

Walter Gage is remembered by Craigdarroch students for the 'merry nonsense' he brought to his mathematics classes.

The First 'Battle of Craigdarroch'

In 1921 when the college moved from the high school, students found their sense of importance 'curiously elevated.' Although they had moved only a few city blocks, they felt a distinctive psychic distance from the classrooms of Victoria High School. No longer tied to their high school years, they now felt like genuine college students, but they belonged to a college whose separate identity was so new that it was without traditions. They soon set about correcting that unhappy state.

By 1923 freshman hazing had become an established custom. An Initiation Dance, given by the sophomores for the freshmen, was held during the second week of each fall term. After spending a week wearing their jackets backwards and hobbling about in shoes from which the shoelaces had been removed, the freshman were put through the final indignity of being smeared with grease paint and dressed in sacks by the sophomores who patrolled the entrances to the ballroom. By 1927 the rites of the Initiation Dance had been refined. Now freshmen were barred from all but the basement entrance to the castle where they were man-handled into submission, decorated with grease-paint, soaked with water, blindfolded and dragged through tunnels in the castle's dungeon-like lower reaches, and forced to eat 'weird concoctions' before being allowed to clean up and find their way upstairs to the dance. 'The Sophs were in their element, maltreating the frightened, innocent Freshie,' the Annual chortled.

By 1929 the tradition had become so well established that it lacked any element of surprise and one particular freshman who was neither frightened, nor innocent of hazing techniques, took advantage of the sophomores' lack of inventiveness to organize the freshman revolt that became known as the 'Battle of Craigdarroch.'[92] Robert Knight was 'a bespectacled rugby forward' who had spent the first week cheerfully wearing the green tie and starched wing-collars required of all the men in his freshman class, but all the while he was carefully plotting the downfall of the second year men. Earning a reputation for

[92] A.C. Young, 'The Battle of Craigdarroch' (typescript, VCCA)

The required dress during Frosh Week, which in this case included the wearing of odd shoes, trousers tucked into socks and the carrying of umbrellas, was a minor indignity compared to what the freshmen experienced on the night of the Initiation Dance.

'military genius,' he explained his analysis of the situation to awed classmates. Freshmen outnumbered sophomores two to one, he pointed out, but the sophomores had two advantages — they were organized and on the night of the Initiation Dance they would be in possession of the castle. At a secret council of war, Knight revealed his strategy. On the evening of the dance, freshmen would lie in ambush at every driveway and pathway that led to the castle. As each sophomore approached, he would be abducted and stashed away in a secret hiding place. Then the freshmen would mass together for an attack on the castle.

"We were all aware of mysterious Sophomore preparations going on in a closely guarded inner sanctum at the east end of the main corridor,' one of Knight's henchmen recalled. 'But under the direction of Knight's council, secret counter-preparations were simultaneously going forward. An air of mystery and suspense hung like a pall over Craigdarroch.'

Several cars and a truck were moved into position. Hand-cuffs and lengths of rope were collected and held in readiness. And a near-by garage, converted into an armory, was stocked with boxes of over-ripe fruit and cartons of eggs.

'By six in the evening unwary sophs were being pounced upon, bound and gagged, trundled into cars and driven off to a holding unit some miles away,' a combatant recalled. When the abandoned cow-barn in the Saanich countryside held a satisfactorily large number of the enemy, Knight called on his troops to regroup, to arm themselves and to prepare for a massed attack on the castle which, he calculated, was being held by as few as two dozen sophs.

Over one hundred freshmen stormed up the stairs, swept across the verandah and hurled themselves against the castle's great west doors. And the freshmen discovered that Knight's plans had two fatal flaws. Each freshman had been directed to arm himself with as many tomatoes, oranges, watermelons, grapefruit and eggs as he could carry. 'It is not easy to hurl one's weight against a door with a pocketful of eggs and tomatoes,' an attacker ruefully recalled. Even had they been empty handed, the freshman would have found themselves meeting an all-but-immovable object, for Knight had failed to account for the whereabouts of one 250-pound rugby forward. He was a member of that small band of castle defenders and he had agreed to act as a doorstop.

Rather than pushing aside resistance and arriving in the hall en masse, the attackers managed to force the door open only a foot or two. They had to be content with laying a barrage of fruit and eggs into the void and satisfied with the knowledge that most of the freshman class escaped the planned hazing.

'Perhaps the most exciting event of the year was the initiation of the freshmen by the sophomores, which proved a very difficult task,' the college Annual dead-panned.

Still bearing its hospital designation Ward 2, Joan Dunsmuir's second floor sitting room served as the Men's Common Room. Here an habitue of the common room enjoys one of the comfortable chairs for which Ward 2 was famous.

The 'Battle of Craigdarroch' lasted less than an hour, and freshmen and sophomores were soon at peace but the reparations exacted by the administration were costly. Judge Gregory must be sent an apology for trespassing on his lawn. A student work-party must clean up the mess. And no longer would freshman hazing be allowed at Victoria College. Judge Gregory was appeased. Six months later there were still egg stains on the hall panelling and melon seeds clinging to the walls above the staircase. And students found other excuses for doing battle.

Still bearing its hospital designation WARD 2 rather ominously stencilled on its door, the Men's Common Room was located in a large second floor room, graced by three of the castle's most exquisite stained glass windows. Male students who smoked were relegated to WARD 9 hidden away along a back hallway in the servants' wing of the third floor. Gradually Ward 9 developed a mystique of its own. What went on in there, female students wondered, as they crept past Ward 9 through the haze of tobacco smoke on their way to the Women's Common Room.

Finally in 1935 the Annual revealed some of Ward 9's secrets. 'The Statistical Bureau shows that there has been an average attendance of twenty-three dyed-in-the-nicotine smokers,' the Annual reported. That figured included 'the one steady pipe- smoker, the two spasmodic pipe-smokers, and the lone but courageous cigar-smoker.' Occupants of Ward 9 whiled away happy hours arguing, cadging cigarettes, aiming wads of paper at wastepaper baskets and when the mood was upon them, indulging in 'community singing' that was 'enjoyed by everyone within a radius of seven blocks.'

For a time the smokers had accepted with equanimity the spartan simplicity of Ward 9 but eventually they came to envy the more luxurious surroundings enjoyed by the denizens of the Men's Common Room. 'Ward 2 is financed by Moscow gold,' the smokers grumbled as they prepared plans to distribute the wealth more equitably. They began by staging a midnight raid to liberate a comfortable leather chair from Ward 2. Then they braced themselves for the expected retaliation. The battle, when it came, was fully covered by war correspondents from *The Microscope*, the college newspaper launched in 1938.[93]

Pierre Berton and 'The Fiend of Craigdarroch'

'For the first time in the history of this institution a new innovation has taken place,' the editors of the *Microscope* proudly and redundantly declared as they announced the birth of the college newspaper. The *Microscope* had noble goals. It would 'rewake the spirit that once animated the students to great achievement.' It would 'publish, each week, club activities' and it would 'raise athletic enthusiasm.' But first the Mike's staff had to grapple with matters of true importance, like experimenting with the motto that would run under the paper's masthead. For a time the front page proudly boasted, 'The Microscope — Magnifies Everything. Tells Nothing.' A few months later the motto read, 'Magnifies All. Prints Anything. Tells Nothing.' Refreshed by the Christmas break, the *Microscope* returned bearing its final and definitive motto — 'No News Is Good News' — and a clear statement of

[93] The *Microscope* was pinned to a notice board where it collected editorial comments and graffiti. Only one or two copies were made of each issue but fortunately a complete set has been preserved in Special Collections, University of Victoria.

its publishing policy. 'Reporters are sent snooping around the College to unearth the goriest, choicest, and most sensational news story possible. This is headlined.' Words to live by, at least for Pierre Berton, one of the Mike's principal perpetrators.

Pierre Berton's name is familiar to most Canadians. A newspaper columnist for large Vancouver and Toronto dailies, a perennial panel-member on C.B.C. television's long-running 'Front Page Challenge,' Berton is also Canada's best known popular historian, whose books invariably rise to the top of almost every year's best-seller lists. Other graduates of Victoria College went on to distinguished careers in the military, in academe and in politics and business, but Berton certainly ranks as the student who has become the most widely known.

'The tallest red-headed man at the college,' Berton was just eighteen when he joined the Mike's staff as the newspaper's cartoonist. With energetic sketches, he lampooned everything from man-hungry co-eds to the Mike's staff itself. But his most famous creation was Gridley Quayle, ace detective.

In a serial story, 'THE CURSE OF THE COLLEGE,' which Berton wrote and illustrated, trench coat-clad Gridley Quayle searched for the 'Fiend of Craigdarroch.' To no one's surprise the Fiend was run to earth in Ward 9.

Pierre Berton
ART EDITOR

Described as 'the tallest red-headed man at Victoria College,' Pierre Berton had other claims to fame. The art director of the Annual, he was also cartoonist, story writer and reporter for the college newspaper, the *Microscope*.

Chapter 1. 'TRAPPED BY THE FIEND'

Synopsis of preceding chapters:

Gridley Quayle, a super snoop, gets word that the fiend he is tracking is lurking in a certain College. Accordingly Quayle disguises himself as a college student (by placing an enormous pipe between his teeth and a tattered copy of Maupassant under his arm). With a flask of College Spirit in his hip pocket, Quayle is prepared.

Now read on:

All was silent in the College as Quayle entered, save for a subdued murmur coming from the direction of the library . . . Suddenly a piercing shriek rent the air, but Gridley Quayle was unperturbed. He knew the Glee Club was rehearsing.

Continuing silently up the stairs, the detective trip-

This sketch of the intrepid detective, who tracked the 'Fiend' to Ward 9, was drawn by Berton to illustrate his serial story.

ped on the inert body of a discarded SCM guest speaker. Then he realized the fiendish power of the Monster he was pursuing . . .

It was then that he saw a Ward 9er going up the stairs to its lair, dragging its pipe behind it. But when Quayle saw that the Creature had an exam paper under its arm, he realized something was wrong.

Springing up the stairs, Quayle dashed into Ward 9. But the room was empty. Too late Gridley Quayle heard the door slam behind him. Too late he heard the evil cackle of the Fiend outside. Too late he saw the dreaded smoke fumes circling around him. Gridley Quayle was trapped.

Chapter 2. 'THE FATE THAT IS WORSE THAN DEATH'

Gridley Quayle was going down for the third time, in fact his nose was just sinking beneath the ashes, when suddenly he remembered the flask of College Spirit in his hip pocket. Raising it to his lips, he drained it, hicoughed (sic) twice, rose to his feet, and seizing an opportunity which lay in a corner, he battered down the door with it, to fall into the arms of Professor Barr, professor of European mystery. With great presence of mind Quayle shouted. 'I hear that Hitler has annexed Pandora Street.' Professor Barr squealed like a wounded freshman, and clutching a copy of 'Inside Europe' to his bosom, ran to the nearest exit.

And so on.

When Ward 2 decided to attack Ward 9, Berton was there in the dual role of combatant and reporter. The whole thing started innocently enough, with a small article complimenting the smokers on their efforts to make Ward 9 more comfortable. 'The improvements in Ward 9 are proceeding nicely. The boys are decorating the place tastefully with street signs and stop signals.' Ward 2 knew instantly what had prompted the new-found pride in their surroundings. There could now be no doubt that Ward

Appearing in almost every issue of the *Microscope* were Berton cartoons, lampooning everything from female students to the staff of the *Microscope* itself.

Pierre Berton added his name to the growing collection of graffiti on the panelling in the common room. Time had surely erased the memory of his personal addition to the castle's interior decor when he served as Governor of Heritage Canada, the outspoken advocate of the preservation of the country's historic buildings.

2's chair was in Ward 9 and that the smokers were busy providing an appropriate setting in which to display their prize. Rallied by the cry 'Ward 2 must have its leather chair!' the attackers poured out of the Men's Common Room and tumbled up the narrow stairs to Ward 9.

In a story with the banner headline 'HEAVY CASUALTIES ON BOTH SIDES,' the *Microscope* described the battle.

> Leading a flank attack up the back stairway, and operating from a base rumoured to be in Ward 2, J. O'Connell led his suicide squad forward with great gusto. Outnumbered by about 764 to 6, the Ward 9ers immediately laid down a heavy smoke barrage from their pipes and amid heavy coughing and choking the battle was under way.
>
> At this point the Women's Underhand Society served tea and to quote McKeachie, 'I think it was just too lovely.'
>
> . . . both sides suffered terrific setbacks through loss of men. Berton reports that he personally broke 17 arms, and Mickleburgh swears that the blood was 6 inches deep in the back corridor.

No statistics were kept of the number who were rendered *hors de combat* by being 'debagged,' but the pile of trousers heaped in the center of the Women's Common Room, located conveniently next door to Ward 9, was rumoured to have reached record heights.

Within a few weeks, Ward 9 was back to normal, so normal that a Mike reporter decided to hazard a visit. 'I wandered into Ward 9 disguised as a rugby player,' he wrote, 'but committed the unpardonable sin of leaving the door open. A storm of protest followed, above which could be heard the authoritarian voice of Doug Worthington. "Shut the door," he screamed. "You'll let the smoke out."'

Ward 9ers, armed with pipes and cigars, gather on Fort Street. Doug Worthington of the authoritarian voice is on the right.

'A Castle for Dunsmuir. A Fire-Trap for Us'

The castle survived the fire that started in Ward 9. 'The fire was discovered by a student who happened to be sitting on top of it,' the *Microscope* explained. It survived the flooding of the upper hallway which resulted when volunteer firemen forgot to attach the hose to the faucet. 'Ward 9 was destroyed by fire and water,' the *Microscope* reported with wishful exaggeration. The castle survived the 'Battle of Craigdarroch'; it survived dances, pep rallies and assorted hi-jinks, including the careful placement of a small car on the entrance roof. But it threatened to burst apart at the seams in 1946 when enrolment, which had seldom reached more than 250, rose to include over 600 students, many of them returning to war-postponed studies, encouraged and financed by the Department of Veterans' Affairs.

Problems had begun the preceding year, when 128 returning servicemen had increased enrolment to more than 400. 'There is not one square inch that is not being used for classroom or study purposes,' the college principal complained.[94] 'There is no kitchen and no dining room this year. They are now classrooms. Into the kitchen have been put rough plank tables and kitchen chairs for the students to sit on . . . There are no locker rooms. They are classrooms this year too, and lockers are scattered all over the building, under stairways, in corners along the hall.'

In 1946, when an additional two hundred students had squeezed themselves into the castle, the situation was even worse. 'Army tables and benches were used to provide additional desks, and sometimes it was hard to squeeze past the door and find a seat,' one student recalled. 'Some of the rooms were so packed with tables and benches that I can remember a number of students, after entering the classroom, having to walk over desk tops to get to their seats.'[95]

'Conditions were intolerable,' another student recalled. 'The halls were so crowded that when you left your classroom you had to move with the flow. If you wanted to go to a classroom on

icated at rough wooden benches, reminiscent of pioneer schoolday n the backwoods, are seen a group of students at Victoria Colleg t the opening of a new term this morning. This was formerly th itchen at the college, and is floored with cold, hard tile. There ar o kitchen or cafeteria facilities for students this year as ever room available is needed for classrooms.

Overcrowding became a real problem at the castle in 1945 and 1946 when enrolment at the college was more than doubled by returning veterans. Every room, including the kitchen, was pressed into service as classroom space. (*Times*, September 20, 1945)

[94] 'Cold Welcome for Students at Vic. College,' undated newspaper clipping, (Gage Collection, Special Collections, University of Victoria)

[95] Dr. R.H. Roy, 'A Long Look Over My Shoulder,' *The Torch* (summer, 1983, VCCA)

The army surplus hut, moved onto the grounds in 1946, was to be converted into two classrooms. It was sited on the terrace behind the annex which had been built during the castle's hospital years to house rehabilitation workshops and which was serving as chemistry and biology labs. (*Times*, September 7, 1946)

Move R.C.A.F. Hut For College Classrooms

The R.C.A.F. hut which is to be converted into two classrooms for Victoria College comes over the wall to rest on the campus. From here it was moved around to the side of the college building, and today the movers put it down two terraces behind the biology building, where it will remain. In order to get it over the low college wall, 4,000 feet of timber was used to build a ramp. The building was jacked up and gradually the truck hauled it up over the obstacle. A smaller building may be acquired for conversion into staff offices, according to Dr. J. M. Ewing, College principal.

LATEST Steel Strikers To Consider Peace Proposals Sunday

your left but the traffic was moving from left to right, then you went with the flow often all the way outside and then tried to catch your classroom on the next pass.'

Craigdarroch was seen as squalidly overcrowded rather than idiosyncratically charming. The castle was 'an inconvenient old dump,' one student grumbled. To Fire Chief Joseph Raymond, the building was more than inconvenient; it was downright dangerous. If a fire occurred many of the students would not get out, Raymond warned. The college principal agreed with the fire chief. 'I can't see that there would be any hope of getting either students or staff out in the event of a fire,' he said. ' The staff members would undoubtedly stay and try and get the young people out and we'd all perish — God help us.'[96]

If visions of at least fifty students trampled to death in the castle's narrow hallways weren't bad enough, the City Health Department decided to condemn the building on quite different grounds. The overcrowding of the building constituted a health hazard,

[96] *Victoria Times*, October 8, 1946

(*Times*, October 8, 1946)

the department warned, pointing out that eight lavatories for 450 male students and four for 150 women couldn't begin to meet even the most minimal health standards.

The solution seemed clear. The college should be moved out of Craigdarroch and onto the campus of the Normal School which had been used as a military hospital during the Second World War and now stood invitingly empty. But while Victoria College continued to be administered by the Greater Victoria School Board, the Normal School was a provincial institution, run by the Depart-

The protest march was organized by student president Terry Garner. A veteran of the R.C.A.F. when he attended Victoria College, Garner later became well-known host on C.B.C. television. (*Times*, October 9, 1946)

ment of Education, and the department had decided that the 115 students enroled in teacher training should be returned to their former home. Perhaps, the government mused, it might be possible to hold some of the college courses in the empty Normal School classrooms.

'A two mile walk between classes?' students asked incredulously. 'Yes,' said the student president, R.C.A.F. veteran Terry Garner. 'We will hold a route march to the Normal School when we have to change classes.'[97]

'Now that gentlemanly negotiations have fallen through and this is what they think is their final offer, it is time for us to take a hand,' Garner announced as he rallied students for the college's first organized protest.

On October 9, 1946 the entire student body, summoned by the ringing of the fire-bell, assembled to begin what must rank as one of the most unusual protest marches ever staged. 'There were so many veterans in it that most of the students marched in step!' And leading the column was piper, Doug Leask, who had piped the Scottish Canadian Regiment onto the beaches of Normandy.[98]

Carrying placards which read 'A Castle for Dunsmuir — A Fire Trap for Us' and 'Will the Government Fiddle While the College Burns,' the students paraded down Fort Street, on to Government Street and past the Empress Hotel to the lawns of the legislative buildings where they were encouraged to spread throughout the city to begin collecting signatures on a petitions

[97] *Victoria Times,* October 9, 1946
[98] Roy, *Torch*

Victoria College students marched down Government Street past the Empress Hotel on their way to the legislative buildings. The sign they are carrying which reads 'Into the College of Death filed the 600' called attention to the dangerously overcrowded conditions that existed at the castle.

to be presented to the premier.

Within days of receiving the petition, signed by almost 20,000 concerned Victorians, the premier, far from unmindful of the political consequences of ignoring veterans' complaints, convened a special cabinet meeting. On October 16th the government reached its decision. The college would be moved out of the castle and would join the student teachers at the Normal School. And the School Board, which had purchased Craigdarroch from the Bank of Montreal in 1929,[99] began to wonder if any earthly use could be found for a condemned castle.

Before long a solution presented itself — Craigdarroch could be used to house the school board staff. And soon the building was transformed into a rabbit's warren of offices.

[99] The School Board acquired title May 8, 1929. Certificate of Indefeasible Title (Land Registry, Victoria)

James Knight Nesbitt and the Second Battle of Craigdarroch

For twenty-one years from 1946 to 1967, the castle served as school board headquarters. The telephone switchboard was moved into the drawing room and while secretaries and superintendents and support staff spread into the basement and over the first three floors, the trustees demonstrated their complete confidence in the sturdiness of the castle by using the fourth floor to solve the weighty problem of text book storage.

During the first years of their occupation the school board staff may have regarded Craigdarroch as little more than a quirky, sometimes charming, often inconvenient home. It took visitors to the city to point out that they were going about their business in a building with compelling appeal.

Violet Wallach moved to the castle in 1955 when her husband was hired to act as the resident custodian. Tucked away in a third floor suite in the servants' wing, the Wallachs enjoyed their accommodations. The view was spectacular. And as Violet recalled with satisfaction, 'We got the best television reception in town up there.'[100]

She had only a few complaints. Hauling her groceries up to the third floor was an unwelcome chore and she wished that the dumb-waiter that ran from the basement up to her suite had not been used to house a tangle of electrical wiring. And she couldn't help but grumble about the fastidious school trustee who objected to her hanging her washing out to dry on lines erected on the castle's lawns. But her most serious problem was lack of privacy. A door separated her suite from the offices that shared the third floor, but the servants' stairs remained open and she often found herself surprised by the arrival of unexpected company.

'I found them one day, Americans they were, and they were picking my cups and saucers out of my china cabinet. I asked them what they were doing and they said, ''Oh, we're just looking at these cups. They must be antique.'' And I said, ''No they're not. They're mine and you're not supposed to be up here.'' '

[100] Mrs. Violet Wallach, Interview, November 8, 1985 (tape, CCA)

Visitors found their way to the castle with no help at all from the school board. The building was not officially open to the public, but even though there were no brochures and no sign posts pointing the way, tourists were drawn to Craigdarroch, their curiosity piqued by the sight of what appeared to be a mysterious fairy tale castle standing high on a hill above the city.

Among Victorians it seemed that only tour bus operators appreciated Craigdarroch's potential. As early as the 1930's drivers had begun to detour from the leafy gardens and wooden mansions of Rockland Avenue to climb the hill to the castle's sandstone magnificence.

'On one tour it would be Lord Dunsmuir who had built Craigdarroch, on another the Duke of Dunsmuir . . . the American tourists really got their money's worth,' one eavesdropper recalled.[101]

It wasn't until 1956, when Victorians began to puzzle over how best to spend the money flowing their way to help them celebrate British Columbia's 1958 centennial, that the first serious suggestions appeared encouraging the city to convert the castle to some tourist-oriented use.

'There's nothing like Craigdarroch castle in North America, except for Casa Loma in Toronto. It would be a wonderful tourist mecca,' enthused Brent Murdoch, a major in the militia who had his eyes firmly fixed on the castle as the site of a military museum.[102]

Echoing Murdoch's appreciation of the building was Chamber of Commerce president Sam Lane. 'Americans are weary of modernism — they come here in search of antiquity,' he said. 'My greatest fear is that we shall pull down our historical landmarks and put up American-type buildings in their place. Craigdarroch Castle is a case in point. It has the making of a first-class attraction for U.S. tourists, yet we use it as an office building.[103]

Supporting Lane's point of view was Victoria businessman Eddy Mallek who had just returned from a three month tour of Europe where he had made the amazing discovery that culture and history could actually become tourist attractions. The restoration of Craigdarroch was 'a must,' Mallek opined.[104]

The school board was not particularly enthralled with all this

[101] Peter Stursberg, *Those Were the Days* (Toronto: Peter Martin, 1969)

[102] *Colonist, June 23, 1956*

[103] *Victoria Times*, December 6, 1957

[104] *Colonist*, December 19, 1957

'Erin Hall' shared Craigdarroch's hill. Built by James Nesbitt's grandfather Samuel Nesbitt in 1873, it was known as 'Cracker Castle' to Victorians who wouldn't let Samuel forget that his fortune had been founded on the manufacture of biscuits. The cow, wandering through the foreground in this photograph, serves as a reminder of the rural nature of upper Fort Street when the castle was constructed.

new interest in the castle. 'If the City wants the building for a museum, the price tag should be $250,000,' trustee Richard Reeve warned.[105] 'The castle is owned by the Greater Victoria School Board. Since taking it over, the board has completed a great many improvements and renovations,' Reeve explained, apparently referring to the lowered ceilings and fluorescent lighting.

For almost ten years Craigdarroch's fate hung in the balance, as debate over its future bounced back and forth between the city and the school board. It was fortunate that during those years of indecison, a castle champion, impatient with civic dithering, stepped forward. James Knight Nesbitt would save the day.

James Nesbitt was uniquely qualified to man the battlements in the castle's defense. He was born in Victoria in 1908, the grandson of biscuit-maker Samuel Nesbitt who had arrived in the city before its incorporation in 1862 and whose home, 'Erin Hall,' had for many years been Craigdarroch's nearest neighbour. Joining the *Victoria Times* as a cub reporter in 1925, 'Jimmy' Nesbitt was referred to as 'the social lion on the *Times* staff' by fellow reporters in recognition of the elevated status he enjoyed as a member of one of the city's 'first families.'

[105] *Victoria Times*, April 4, 1958

As well as socially, Nesbitt was politically well-connected. Assigned to cover the provincial legislature in 1936, he became the grand old man of the press gallery, a position officially acknowledged in 1974 when upon his retirement he was given the signal honour of being named an honorary life member of the gallery.

But more than his social and political connections, his willingness to appear slightly ridiculous for the sake of causes he held dear made him an effective campaigner. 'Eccentrics are a community asset,' Nesbitt claimed.[106] And of course he was talking about himself.

'I'm not saying that everyone should be an eccentric, but it does get results,' he said, recalling that his campaign to have the government spend $1000 marking pioneer graves in Victoria's historic Ross Bay Cemetery had been met with ennui until he had pitched a tent among the tombstones and summoned a *Times* photographer to capture him curling up for the night. That ploy had worked so well that he decided to use a variation on the theme when the public works department announced that mosaic tile flooring in the legislative buildings would be replaced with more practical linoleum. Nesbitt moved in with his sleeping bag and the public works department decided to reconsider the idea.

Nesbitt's reputation for 'strategic wackiness' was such that even would-be enemies reacted with amused sighs as they shook their heads over his more outrageous opinions. Columnist Marjorie Nichols first encountered Nesbitt in 1972 when she came to Victoria to cover the legislature. 'I marched into the press gallery in Victoria and committed the double misdeed of being attired in slacks and of having uttered a word slightly stronger than darn,' she recalled.[107] Later that day a male reporter encountered Nesbitt in the men's washroom. With exaggerated gestures he was peering under the door of each cubicle. Asked what he was up to, Nesbitt harrumphed, 'Just checking to see if that foul woman in pants is in here too.'

A firm believer that a woman's place was in the home, Nesbitt reacted with indignation when it was suggested that girls should be given the opportunity to become legislative pages. They would be "more content happily married, lovingly looking after husbands, children and staying home, singing the old song about

[106] *Colonist*, September 28, 1961
[107] *Vancouver Sun*, September 29, 1981

In 1961 James Nesbitt camped out in the legislative buildings to save them from 'desecration' by an insensitive minister of public works. The stunt was Nesbitt's own idea, but the gun he is holding was the suggestion of *Colonist* photographer Ian McKain who scurried up the street to Robinson's Sporting Goods to borrow it. The gun had once belonged to Richard Blanshard, the first governor of Vancouver Island, the *Colonist* solemnly reported.

the hand rocking the cradle ruling the world,' he blustered.

In 1973 the Vancouver Status of Women Council named him Grand Champion Boar for 'outstanding and consistent service to the cause of male chauvinism.'

'I like to think I have done my small part in making women happier,' Nesbitt burbled.[108]

In 1959 James K. Nesbitt, fifty-one years old, still a working reporter and not quite yet an established eccentric, formed the Castle Preservation Society. And rather than beat the bushes for fellow-enthusiasts, he went straight to the top. That first membership list was so cunning a combination of disparate but influential people that only a person with his connections could have brought them together and only a person with his imagination would have thought to approach them.

The first names on the membership list belonged to Lieutenant

[108] *Vancouver Sun*, February 21, 1973

Governor Frank Ross and his wife Phyllis. Among those joining them were Premier W.A.C. Bennett, Percy Scurrah the mayor of Victoria, Stuart Keate publisher of the *Times*, restoration architect Peter Cotton, and James Audain great-grandson of Robert Dunsmuir.

Rolling up his sleeves, Nesbitt began to pepper politicians with letters asking for clarification of the castle's ownership and demanding that something be done to prevent its crumbling through neglect. The question of ownership became crucial in 1964 when the school board announced that it was planning to vacate the building for more spacious premises. 'Who will asssume responsibility for the castle when the board moves out?' Nesbitt asked, convinced that if the building were left vacant, vandalism would complete the destruction that lack of maintenance had begun.

'Why it's owned by School District 61 — who else?' Alderman Curtis exclaimed impatiently in response to a polite enquiry from the Castle Society. 'Everybody seems to know who owns Craigdarroch but the Castle Society,' city manager Dennis Young quipped.[109]

President of the Castle Society, James Nesbitt conducts a meeting in the castle's drawing room.

Two years later a careful examination of documents determined that the castle did in fact belong to the city, that it had reverted to the city when the City of Victoria Board of School Trustees had ceased to exist and its duties had been assumed by the Greater Victoria School Board. That question having been finally settled, Nesbitt and the Castle Society levelled their guns on the city council and let loose a volley of complaints about Craigdarroch's deteriorating condition.

Some window frames were spongy with rot; slate tiles were sliding from the roof; and sandstone was flaking from the walls. Not having complete confidence in the school board's claim that the castle was being well-maintained, the mayor sent city engineer James Garnett on a tour of inspection. He reported that the building was 'in remarkable condition, considering its age' — a statement guaranteed to provoke a response from Nesbitt.

'Age should have nothing to do with the matter, as long as the building is adequately maintained,' he rumbled. 'What has age to do with St. Paul's or Westminster Abbey? They are as sound as the day they were built, because they are protected and

[109] *Colonist*, December 4, 1966

kept up.'

'Did Mr. Garnett see the holes in the stained-glass or note how the windows bulged? Did he not observe the erosion of the stonework, and the shingles missing on the roof? Did he not see the dirty windows, and the dampness in the porch ceiling or note the huge chunks of missing granite?'[110]

Apparently not. And it seems that Garnett was not moved to take a careful second look for maintenance of the building did not improve during the remaining years of the board's tenancy.

By 1968 when the school board and the castle finally parted company, Victoria's city council had fielded a variety of suggestions regarding Craigdarroch's future use. The land surrounding it was very valuable. Perhaps the castle should be demolished and a high rise apartment building erected in its place. Or then again, perhaps it should be retained and become the home of the provincial premier. Or might Nesbitt be right? Was Craigdarroch a valuable tourist attraction? After all, the visitors' book placed in the castle by the Society had collected a thousand signatures a month during the summer.

Might the castle be worth keeping? Certainly not! At least not according to professor of history, Dr. Sydney Jackman, who described Craigdarroch as 'the greatest white elephant in Victoria.'

'Craigdarroch Castle is Balmoral blown across the Atlantic. Very big, very prominent, very uninteresting,' he declaimed.[111]

But the Victoria School of Music thought Craigdarroch was very interesting indeed. Founded in 1964 and needing a home for its forty staff members and 435 students, the school had been hankering after the castle ever since it heard that it might become available. Perhaps relieved that they could subsidize the school and solve the problem of the castle in one fell swoop, city council decided to lease the building to the musicians for a dollar a year.

As the music school prepared to move in, Nesbitt flew into action. He placed odd bits of furniture collected from friends and Society members here and there in the castle's first floor rooms, trying to make them appear to be much too crowded to accept any of the thirty-five pianos that were beginning to collect in the hall. He succeeded in keeping only the library and the dining room piano-free but they were a beginning, giving visitors at least some space they could call their own.

[110] *Colonist*, February 9, 1968
[111] *Colonist*, March 31, 1966

And visitors continued to appear at the castle in increasing numbers. One April day in 1969 Nesbitt arrived to find it crawling with tourists. 'So I thought to myself, why not see if they are interested in paying for their pleasure,' he recalled.[112] He popped back home and collected a plate and a small table and chair. He set them up at the entrance with a hand-lettered sign reading 'Donations are Welcome.' Returning four hours later, he found that forty-five dollars had accumulated in his kitchen plate. By the end of the year almost five thousand dollars had been donated and Nesbitt began to suspect that if more rooms were available to view and if the castle were open on a regular basis, it might actually be able to pay its own way. But for the time being the music school, which had been transformed into the Conservatory of Music, was the tenant and it showed no inclination to move.

From that April afternoon, scarcely a day passed when the conservatory was not blessed with Nesbitt's presence. Knowing that the Society had no official status at the castle but recognizing that possession was nine-tenths of the law, he became a permanent fixture, writing his newspaper columns hunched over the little desk he set up just inside Craigdarroch's west door where he greeted tourists with a smile and music students with a scowl.

The relationship between Nesbitt and the conservatory quickly became a war of nerves. He liked most of the teachers but he was appalled at the damage he witnessed; the nicks and scratches that appeared on the panelling in the hall and up the staircase and the partitioning of rooms on the upper floors into tiny cubicles, just large enough to enclose a piano. And he took no pains to hide his displeasure. Hard of hearing and with his ears stuffed with cotton wool to combat chronic infections, he spoke much too loudly and people wanting to talk to him would have to raise their voices to a bellow.[113]

A booming voice in the front hall was not especially appreciated by Robin Wood, the conservatory director, who gave piano lessons in the drawing room. But even more irritating was Nesbitt's performance on concert nights. With the drawing room packed with attentive listeners, he would sit at his post, smoke from the cigarette in a half-concealed ashtray curling about his head as he turned the pages of his evening newspaper with theatrical aggressiveness. His response to the stares and admonitions directed

[112] *The Victorian*, October 25, 1972
[113] Bruce Davies, personal communication, March, 1987

Robin Wood, Principal of the Conservatory, (center) with cellist James Hunter (left) and composer and violinist Murray Adaskin.

his way was to grumble and increase the volume of the noise.

Even without Nesbitt's campaign of gentle harrassment, the conservatory's teachers found conducting classes in a tourist attraction rather trying, and sometimes they reacted with unqualified rudeness. In 1976 Hilda Millet, visiting the city from Ontario, dropped in to have a look at Craigdarroch. It would not be a happy experience.[114]

'We spent quite some time in the original study and dining room,' she said. 'But the rest of the castle was a total disaster.'

[114] *Victoria Times*, August 10, 1976

After shaking her head over the chairs and the piano jammed into the drawing room and noting with disapproval the litter of dirty coffee cups in the kitchen, she made her way up the back stairs where she was jostled and bumped by students hurrying to and from music lessons.

Exploring the second floor, she found a confusing array of doors, some closed, some standing ajar and none with any identifying signs. 'The first door at the left at the top of the stairs was closed but had no sign saying it was private or in use,' Hilda explained. 'I was hoping it would be a furnished room and ventured to look in very quietly. Upon opening the door I found myself face to face with a teacher in the process of teaching a class, but before I could excuse myself, the door was literally slammed in my face by the teacher. The bang could be heard throughout the building.'

The only good thing about her visit was the sympathetic hearing she received from 'the gentleman at the front desk,' who one suspects may have had trouble concealing his glee. If teachers were being driven to distraction by interruptions, how much longer could the conservatory continue to tolerate the inconveniences of operating in the castle?

Only as long as it takes to find a new home, the musicians might have answered. In 1979 they persuaded the government to allow them to use a vacant school building and with a relieved sigh they left Craigdarroch. And surely some members of the Castle Society uncorked a bottle of champagne.

Rugby Players Need not Apply

James Nesbitt died on September 27, 1981. He had, as usual, spent the day at the castle before going home to his bachelor digs where sometime during the night he suffered a fatal heart attack. In recounting his career, obituary writers focussed on his role as founder of the Castle Society and Nesbitt would have agreed that the preservation of Craigdarroch had been his greatest accomplishment.

Like Alexander Dunsmuir's San Leandro house and James Dunsmuir's 'Hatley,' Craigdarroch has on several occasions served as a film set. Here comedienne Phyllis Diller pauses in the castle's hall during filming of her television special.

When the conservatory moved out, the city decided to leave the castle in the hands of the Society, and so it remains today. The building continues to be owned by the city but the management and restoration of the building are overseen by an unpaid Board of Trustees elected from the Society's membership. The City of Victoria provides no financial aid; in fact the city bills the Society when city parks crews are employed to trim the lawns. Occasionally the provincial government provides small employment grants or grants for special projects, such as the inventory and inspection of the stained glass windows, but for the most part Craigdarroch is dependent on donations and on the admission fees, instituted in 1986 in an attempt to bring about at least some degree of budgetary predictability.

The castle operates chiefly as a museum entertaining over one hundred thousand visitors a year. But with many expensive restoration projects in limbo due to lack of funds, new ways to generate money are constantly being explored. Fortunately the castle's unique appeal suggests a variety of uses, with the trustees fielding requests from individuals and groups for everything from private parties to commercial events. And while rugby players planning an after-the-game stag party need not apply, the Society seriously considers any suggestion that would not result in damage to the building or its furnishings.

On two occasions the castle has become a film set and on both occasions, the grand staircase was the feature that caught the imagination of the director. Filming her television special, Phyllis Diller drifted down the stairs in a scene recalling Scarlett O'Hara and the ante-bellum South, and during the making of 'Glitterdome' James Garner, playing a Los Angeles police detective, looked up to exchange significant glances with Margot Kidder who appeared to great advantage standing on the landing surrounded by the glow of polished golden oak.

The director of 'Glitterdome' Stuart Margolin, perhaps best known for his role as Angel in the 'Rockford Files,' put practical considerations aside to film at Craigdarroch. 'The drawing room really wasn't big enough for the party scene and we didn't get to use many of the extras we hired . . . but that hall and that staircase . . . I couldn't resist using them.'[115]

Dorothy Laundy, who for many years had served as James

[115] Stuart Margolin, personal communication, March 1987

Nesbitt's right hand woman and who was continuing to act as the castle's most vigilant watch dog found the film crews almost more trouble than they were worth. 'They used real food in the dining room scene and real wine too, I think. I had to watch every move they made and one fellow became very unpleasant when I told him not to put his glass down on the buffet.'[116]

More welcome are the brides who come to Craigdarroch to be married. And proving that everyone gets caught up in the excitement and romance of weddings, tourists willingly obey the sign reading 'Quiet Please. Wedding in Progress' attached to the drawing room door.

Perhaps the most successful event ever held at the castle was 'Christmas at Craigdarroch' first staged by the Junior League in 1984. With the spicy scent of pine and cedar filling the air and with every decorated room glinting with lights and baubles, Craigdarroch welcomed thousands of visitors as residents of Victoria, usually blase about the castle in their midst, almost overwhelmed the organizers in their eagerness to see the League's interpretation of a Victorian Christmas.

For many it was their first visit to the castle, but their imagination captured by the building as much as by the decorations, many returned for a leisurely tour and the Society noted with delight that attendance figures during the usually slack off-season months had begun to climb.

Today no one would suggest that the castle be demolished. And it is becoming increasingly popular with Victorians who are beginning to appreciate what tourists have always known — Craigdarroch is a civic treasure. But the struggle to maintain the building continues. Roof slates need replacement; the problem of deteriorating sandstone must be solved; the building must conform to increasingly stringent fire codes. And in the meantime, many restoration projects must be postponed. Partition walls, lowered ceilings, fluorescent lighting and other 'improvements' made by the Department of Soldiers' Civil Re-establishment, by the School Board and by the Conservatory have been removed. But Joan Dusnmuir's second floor suite is still divided by a ladies washroom and many coats of institutional paint still cover the hand-painted decoration on the drawing room ceiling.

It takes a particular kind of cock-eyed optimism to visualize

[116] Dorothy Laundy, personal communication, April, 1987

the day when Craigdarroch will be fully restored. But then optimism, cock-eyed or otherwise, is the one commodity with which the Castle Society has always been well supplied.

Appendix One

Several pioneer residents of Nanaimo have recorded their reminiscences of Dunsmuir's Nanaimo homes. William Barraclough, in an article based on 'many sources' and published in *Nanaimo Retrospective*, states that Dunsmuir built a 'log cottage' on Front Street beside the Bastion in 1858. Mark Bate, in a memoir printed in the *Nanaimo Free Press*, February 9, 1907 writes that in 1857 the frame of Robert Dunsmuir's house was awaiting completion, but he places this house at the corner of Albert and Wallace and states that while this house was being built, Dunsmuir was living in a log cabin on Front Street.

Barraclough records that in 1869 Dunsmuir built a house on Jingle Pot Road near Wellington and states that the house was named 'Ardoon.' Bate agrees that Dunsmuir built a country house, but applied the name 'Ardoon' to the Dunsmuir house at the corner of Albert and Wallace. J.E.L. Muir and William Lewis, whose reminiscences appear in *Nanaimo Retrospective*, both agree that Dunsmuir lived in Nanaimo, rather than at Wellington, and confirm the location as being at Albert and Wallace. It would seem more likely that the name 'Ardoon' was applied to Dunsmuir's principal residence. Bate clearly states (*Nanaimo Free Press*, February 23, 1907) that this was so and he is a particularly convincing witness since he acquired the house after Dunsmuir moved to Victoria.

Appendix Two

During the period of Craigdarroch's construction, it was not unusual for both Victoria newspapers to run full descriptions of the larger houses that had been built during any given year. Those descriptions usually included a list of all the tradesmen involved and invariably included the building's total cost. That this did not occur in the case of Craigdarroch has been attributed to Dunsmuir's desire for secrecy, to his reluctance to let his employees know just how much he had to spend. But this seems unlikely. If an American contractor, form Portland or from San Francisco, was used and given that the architects were not local men, there was little incentive for the newspapers to publish full reports, as those reports were simply a form of civic boosterism.

The lack of published information about the castle has made even so simple a question as its cost a difficult one to answer.

Brief mention of the Dunsmuir residence was made each year in annual summaries of all construction that had taken place in the city.

1887 — $ 10,000	for work on foundation, *Times*, December 31, 1887
1888 — $165,000	for work on new residence and improvement to grounds, *Times*, December 27, 1888
1889 — $150,000	for work on residence during year, *Colonist*, January 1, 1890
1890 — $ 53,000	work done this year to residence, *Colonist*, January 1, 1891

The total of these annual statements is $370,000, but of course this did not include the cost of the land, nor of any finishing touches such as the stained glass windows.

Occasionally reporters hazarded a guess at what the total cost might be.

'The palatial residence when completed will cost in the neighbourhood of $500,000 and will be the finest on the Pacific Coast outside San Francisco.' *Times*, December 27, 1888.

'The palatial residence of Hon. R. Dunsmuir . . . will cost when completed fully $300,000.' *Colonist*, January 1, 1889.

The $500,000 estimate was made the following year in the *Colonist*, January 1, 1891. 'Dunsmuir Castle . . . is among the finest residences on the continent.'

In 1898 the value, rather than the cost, of Craigdarroch became the subject of public comment. Joan contested the $80,000 assessed value the city had placed on Craigdarroch. She successfully had it reduced to $45,000. The standard of evaluation was 'the actual cash value as appraised in payment of a just debt from a solvent debtor' and, as an assessor explained, 'it was a very expensive building and no one in Victoria would accept it in payment of a debt.' During the hearing, the city assessor suggested that the castle had cost $185,000 to build. (*Colonist*, August 7, 1898)

Abbreviations

CCA	Craigdarroch Castle Archives
OHS	Oregon Historical Society
PABC	Provincial Archives of British Columbia
VCA	Victoria City Archives
VCCA	Victoria College Craigdarroch Archives

Bibliography

Newspapers

Nanaimo Free Press
Portland Oregonian
Vancouver Sun
Vancouver Province
Victoria Colonist
Victoria Times

Books and Articles

Audain, James. *From Coalmine to Castle*. New York: Pageant Press, 1955.

Hawkins III, William J. 'Warren Heywood Williams, Architect (1884 - 1888).' *Portland Friends of Cast-Iron Archietecture Newsletter*, December, 1980.

Lewis, Oscar. *The Big Four*. New York: Alfred A. Knopf, 1959.

Morton, James. *In the Sea of Sterile Mountains. The Chinese in British Columbia*. Vancouver: J.J. Douglas, 1974.

Norcross, E. Blanche (ed.). *Nanaimo Retropsective. The First Century*. Nanaimo: Nanaimo Historical Society, 1979.

Phillips, Paul. *No Power Greater: A Century of Labour in British Columbia*. Vancouver: B.C. Federation of Labour, 1967.

Reksten, Terry. *'More English Than the English.' A Very Social History of Victoria*. Victoria, Orca Books, 1986.

Smith, Peter L. *Come Give A Cheer! One Hundred Years of Victoria High School 1867 - 1967*. Victoria: Victoria High School Centennial Celebrations Committee, 1976.

Stursberg, Peter. *Those Were the Days*. Toronto: Peter Martin, 1969.

Turner, Robert. *Vancouver Island Railroads*. San Marino: Golden West Books, 1981.

Terry Reksten's talent for making history come alive is once again confirmed with *Craigdarroch: The Story of Dunsmuir Castle.*

Terry's first book, *Rattenbury* (Sono Nis Press, 1978) won the Eaton's Literary Award. *"More English that the English" — A Very Social History of Victoria* (Orca Book Publishers, 1986) was an almost-instant local bestseller.